Reawakening The Spirit In Work

Jack Hawley

A FIRESIDE BOOK
Published by Simon & Schuster
New York London Toronto Sydney Tokyo Singapore

FIRESIDE
Rockefeller Center
1230 Avenue of the Americas
New York, New York 10020

First Fireside Edition 1995
Published by arrangement with Barrett-Koehler Publishers, Inc.

Manufactured in the United States of America

10 9 8 7 6 5 4 3 2 1

Library of Congress Cataloging-in-Publication Data

Hawley, John A., date.
   Reawakening the spirit in work / Jack Hawley.—1st Fireside ed.
      p.   cm.
   "A Fireside book."
   Includes bibliographical references and index.
   1. Leadership—Moral and ethical aspects.   2. Management—Moral and ethical aspects.
3. Dharma.   4. Spiritual life.   I. Title.
HD57.7.H39   1995
658.4'092—dc20   94-29599 CIP

ISBN 0-671-88522-7

Dedicated with full heart
to Sri Sathya Sai Baba

Nicholas Roerich, *Kanchenjunga*, 1924

Tempera on canvas, 27½ by 42½ in.

Nicholas Roerich (1874–1947), the Russian master painter/writer/ humanitarian/Nobel Peace Prize candidate, lived the last two decades of his life in the Kulu Valley in northern India. He devoted all of his energies to his fervent belief that art has a beneficial effect on the spirit of the world. His hundreds of Himalayan landscapes draw our eyes and hearts upward toward the citadel of the spirit. In his writings Roerich often refers to the vast riches stored within the Himalayas.

Kanchenjunga literally means the Five Treasures of the Great Snows—the most precious of which is the wisdom that dwells deep within us. I am grateful to Dr. Svetoslav Roerich in Bangalore and Mr. Daniel Entin, Director of the Nicholas Roerich Museum in New York, for permission to use this painting.

CONTENTS

PREFACE

I started out to write a straightforward management book about how to transform organizations, but the deeper I dove into the ocean of questions facing managers nowadays, the more profound the issues were. Ultimately, I found myself plunged into the big questions of life: What's it all about? Is what I do in life of any value? How might I live a fuller life both on and off the job?

These were deep subjects that came from delving into management with a particular attitude. Dive deeply enough into any subject and the questions that shimmer before you are spiritual.

IT'S ABOUT WHAT IT'S ALL ABOUT

This book is about human spirit, respect, and dignity—things that have mattered to me throughout my working life, and are mattering to more and more other people these days. It's also about living life gracefully, about living a full life, about being more alive while we're here. This is not a treatise on retreating to a monastery or retiring into nature; rather, it's about making the most of this journey and living a higher, better life. It's even about being a hero.

The spiritual journey is a personal, inner experience. You can try to explain spirituality, but the hollow echoes of the descriptions tend to hang around in people's minds, not quite making it to their hearts. The only way to really come to spirit is to experience it. Relating metaphorical incidents (stories) is a more, well, experiential way of conveying spirit. From stories, we each get what we need at that moment rather than what the speaker or teacher might have in mind for us. Although I'm a little shy about the personal vignettes that occasionally pop up in these pages, I've decided to include them—not to lay out any particular ideology or path but to help readers experience these things themselves and make their own way.

THE NEW PARADIGM

We don't have to spend much time talking about the great changes happening in the world today. We've all seen the graphs where change is curving straight upward after having been essentially flat for eons.

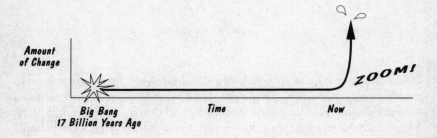

Among the huge changes zooming at us are some fundamentally new recipes for comprehending the world of management and leadership. It's as if this new management chemistry were coming together on the stove in front of our very noses. Wafting from this concoction are some rather mysterious aromas that arise from stirring in things like spirit, heart, and energy—ingredients we've not had much experience with before.

This book contains several of the more recognizable elements from this new stew. Some of them began to emerge a few years ago during an impromptu eighteen-month symposium, when I and seven other consultants from the Los Angeles area journeyed deep into the human heart of transformation. Our original purpose was to put "Organization Transformation" on the agenda of a national conference for the first time. To do that right, we had to delve into the topic ourselves.

Even though we didn't see ourselves as pilgrim types, the delving became a spiritual journey. Why? Because that's what real transformation is: a spiritual expedition. We discovered that when you search for the soul of any idea you have to enter into your own soul. Aha, we discovered that we are all pilgrims—and that our journeys are ever continuing and ever more exciting.

ACKNOWLEDGMENTS

Thanks to the core Organization Transformation group in Los Angeles for the memories and for being in on the beginning of many of these ideas: Beverly Adante, Sam Farry, Louise Hawley, Joseph Reyes, Charles Schaefer, and Tuck Taylor. And thanks to the twenty or so others for occasionally being there.

Thank you, Dean Lused, for being the instrument that jolted this book beyond a series of lectures.

Special thanks to Tony Rose for being so interested in words, and to Dom Cirin and Robin James for being so available for comments and re-actions.

Thank you, Joy Thomas, Barbara Bozzani, Mary Keane, Dyan Ellebracht, Christal Kerrigan, Sheryl Politiski, for being ready to react so encouragingly to various parts of this work and for prepublishing some sections of it.

Thank you, Bob Ahern, for being a yeoman, and Sunny, for the gift of *Standards*—and to Erick Henriksen and Judy Brecher, for being at our faraway place when I most needed technical help with the computer.

Thank you, Roxanne Morgan, for bringing us to tea with Dr. Svetoslav Roerich in Bangalore, and for being there with us.

Thanks to the scores of people from all over the world for being so instantly receptive to the idea of this book. Your swiftly positive reactions have sustained it more than you realize.

Thanks to the many managers at all levels with whom I have worked who have repeatedly shown me that dharmic management can work.

Thank you, Jack Forem, for being ready to get to the heart of things in the early draft; and thank you, Lila Youngs, for being the bump-smoother of the critical middle draft.

Thank you, V.K. Narasimhan, for your unique perspectives and good-natured comments—and for being a fellow toiler in the garden.

Thanks to the four Berrett-Koehler reviewers for being there at the right time with your great ideas: George Morrisey, Chris Largent/Denise Breton, and Jennifer Myers; and thanks to the whole B-K group for being a great team.

Thank you, offspring and families, Kathy, Jason, Adam, Tom, Alec, Owen, April, Julie, and Rich, for being so understanding and encouraging during all the months I was in a "cave" writing.

Thank you, Louise, for being so truly *with* me as we again learned so much together during this project. Your "feeding the author," as you put it, provided nourishment for the soul; your unflagging, restless impatience kept the book earthbound, and your loving patience with me kept me earthbound.

And finally, ultimately, thank you, Swami, for *being* me—every breath and every moment.

January 1993   Jack Hawley
Prasanthi Nilayam
India

THE AUTHOR

For thirty years Jack Hawley has been involved in some of the more successful programs for organization effectiveness. For over twenty years he has been the president of his own management consulting firm and founder of a consortium of consultants. His company works with clients (usually large private and government organizations) to improve their productivity and create better working environments. Emphasis in these programs is on truth, on facing up, on infusing new energy, heart, and spirit—and on making lasting changes in organization life-style.

Prior to consulting, Hawley spent ten years as an executive in the high-technology and service industries (Hotel Corporation of America and TRW Space Technology Labs). His graduate work was done at Cornell University in Industrial and Labor Relations, and at Columbia Pacific University. He holds a doctoral degree in organization behavior and has taught part-time at several universities (Cornell, Pepperdine, University of California, Riverside).

A number of years ago Hawley's search for a deeper experience of life took him to India to learn new powers at the feet of a famous holy man. Now he spends one half of each year in an ashram in southern India and the other half consulting with top executives in Europe and the United States. This requires stepping from a dusty little town in India to the large cities in the West, from the hut to the boardroom, from sandals to polished shoes—a continuing leap from the thicket to the thick of it.

Why India? It's part of the leap. India bequeaths the priceless gift of more time and space. It opens the door to a vast storehouse of jewel insights and ancient/new ideas. It offers a quieter, simpler life with time for burrowing into crucial matters like spirituality and character in day-to-day living—done in an atmosphere saturated with learning and dedicated to applying that learning in daily life. This book, *Reawakening the Spirit in Work,* grew out of a series of lectures on organization transformation presented by Hawley at the ashram university in India.

Hawley and his wife, Louise, live in Southern California and Mexico. Their five grown offspring and their families reside throughout the United States, from Florida to Hawaii.

Jack Hawley may be reached through John A. Hawley Associates, c/o Parkside Management, 806 Manhattan Beach Blvd., Manhattan Beach, CA 90266; telephone: (310) 376-5448.

INTRODUCTION

GOING HOME TO SPIRIT AND CHARACTER IN THE WORKPLACE

The key questions for today's managers and leaders are no longer issues of task and structure but are questions of spirit. This book reaches beyond the usual management issues straight into the new paradigm, into the new way of thinking about life itself and about being a manager or leader.

Why this book? To help counter the erosion of spirit and the pattern of thoughtless dishonesty that are sweeping the world these days. The book's primary aim is to feed the roots of integrity and nudge toward spirit.

The word *dharmic* is Sanskrit for deep, deep integrity—living by your inner truth. *Dharmic management* means bringing that truth with you when you go to work every day. It's the fusing of spirit, character, human values, and decency in the workplace and in life as a whole.

This book is a nonreligious, squarely spiritual management book— to my knowledge the first of its kind. It's about the things we're all concerned about: purpose and meaning, peace (inner peace, especially), health, happiness, love, life, and death. It's about being powerful. It's

1

about Truth. It's about making the most of the heartbeats you've been given. It's about caring more and carrying on.

This book comes to grips with some of the life questions that have exploded into the world's consciousness over the past few years. Questions about happiness. Basic questions of the soul that reflect shaken beliefs in the way things are in the world. Questions about personal emptiness, coming out of people's hunger for more integrity in their day-to-day lives. Questions, then, about how to muster the energy and courage to face those lives. And, inevitably, queries of life's meaning itself, of death, and of birth.

A BOOK FOR EVERYBODY

This is a spiritual adventure book which uses management as the window on the world. It's told through the management window because, well, that's my particular viewing place, and management happens to be the window of today. Our culture is so steeped in management that everybody talks and understands the language. When I speak to groups of nonmanagers, I don't worry anymore whether they'll understand my words, they all do. It wasn't only MBAs who were reading Peters and Waterman's (1982) "management" book *(In Search of Excellence)*; homemakers, teachers, and taxi drivers—all of whom have a lot to manage—were getting a lot out of it too. It is through that opening we launch the inner adventure.

This then is a book for everybody who feels the gnawing hunger for something more in the world, for a world with more integrity in it. I especially hope that managers and leaders get something out of it.

Speaking to a Need

> A *Time* magazine cover story deals with the "malformations cropping up in the American character," and calls this an era of "self-absorbed individualism."

> The *Los Angeles Times* reports on a meeting of the Dalai Lama with a group of high-level American business leaders—true moguls of industry. Their most often asked question is, How can we introduce more ethics and spirituality into our businesses and everyday lives?

In a *Fortune* survey, Americans with six-figure incomes
were asked to list their heroes. Mother Teresa was one
of the most often mentioned. Her name appears along
with Iacocca and Einstein.

Life magazine tells of the personal transformation of a
tough (some say mean-spirited) political-campaign
battler who is dying of cancer. "I sense that something is
stirring in American society," he says from his hospital
room, "something crucial is missing from people's lives;
there's a spiritual vacuum at the heart of American
society." Later he refers to it as "a tumor of the soul."

Many others are talking and writing about "the moral
erosion" that is distressing people everywhere these
days.

What's coming through here? It's the call of purpose, meaning, and
character in life and in business life. It's the call of Spirit. And this call must
be handled. There's no answering machine for this one. Turn the bell to
"soft" if necessary, but carefully and respectfully pick up the receiver and
reply. The stakes are high. The way the call is answered will set the fullness
or emptiness of life from today onward.

This call of Spirit isn't only for individuals. It's ringing up entire
organizations, professions, even the whole planet. Not only poets and
philosophers but also hard scientists and hard-nosed businesspeople
are learning that their life queries are, in the upper reaches, spiritual.
These are times when humankind is being called to those upper
reaches.

SPIRITUALITY, NOT RELIGION

This is a spiritual book, not a religious book. What's the difference?
To put it simply: spirituality is the goal, religion is the path. I gave
an assignment to a class of bright MBA students at the university in India,
asking them to help me tease apart religion and spirituality. A few got
it mixed up, as many of us do; most were of great help. Here's the gist:

Religion	Spirituality
Product of a certain time and place	The goal, more than the path
Meant for a group	Meant for the individual; a personal, private journey
Focuses more on the path to the goal; prescribed codes of conduct	Contains elements common to all religions (love, belief, golden rule, and so forth)
A system of thought	An adventure, moving toward one's source
A set of beliefs, rituals, and ceremonies to help you progress along the path	A state, beyond the senses (beyond even thought)
Institutions and organizations	Inquiry into true Self
A community for sharing life's burdens and joys	The transition from uncertainty to clarity
A way of life	

A new kind of spiriting is afoot these days. More and more, as Lucy Cornelssen (1986) talks about in her book, individuals will be called to face the beyond within themselves—without a priest, without a church, without ceremonies—simply within their own nature, all alone. This is a book of these new-spiriting times. It's about the list on the right.

A basic premise of the book is also essentially a spiritual idea. It's that we already have whatever it is that we really need in this life. This means that we don't have to *become* something; rather, we need to return to a certain mental place, or regain something of quality. Here's how the book unfolds:

Part I, "Respiriting," grounds spirit in an explanation of what it is, how it fits into the new management agenda, and how important it is for us to live in a state of *constant spiritual awareness.* The point: we can, and must, go home again.

Part II, "Revering," addresses a cornerstone spiritual value: deep caring for others—a respect so intense it becomes reverence. We carefully walk up to what love, the "L-word" in business, actually means, and whether or not it is relevant in the workplace.

Part III, "Repowering," considers five powerful ideas:

Belief: brawny belief, conviction, knowing, faith, trust. It's the force that conveys our essence to us.

Thought Power: weaving our thoughts into such a tight pattern that they shape our lives and our organizations.

Already-Thereness: going further into the audacious idea that life is not a matter of trying to become, it's a matter of realizing and being.

Instantaneousness: the daring companion idea that massive personal and organizational change can, and often does, happen in the blink of an eye.

Untethering: the important understanding that true freedom comes from being unhooked, uncaught by the stuff of worldly life. It's about the basic inner power of personal freedom.

Part IV, "Recharactering," is about how to actually live by one's inner truth—an idea even more awesome than freedom. It asserts that character is what makes the recipe of life work, determining whether we gag on life or savor it. The concept of *dharma* is affixed to integrity, drawing to it the energies of rightness, spirit, and fearlessness, creating a sort of superintegrity. A prescription for doing some of this is included.

Finally, Part V, "Reinspiring," helps us understand that all leadership is spiritual because the leader seeks to liberate the best in people and the best is always linked to one's higher self. Thus we come back full circle to spirit, to living by one's inner truth. We learn that when leaders follow their hearts, others rise to those heights.

The appendix, "A Glimpse into the Sathya Sai Baba Phenomenon," offers to the interested or curious more information on Sathya Sai Baba and his teachings.

"BUT BUSINESS IS BOTTOM LINE, BABY!"

This book isn't about spirit and integrity in the ozone of theory; instead, it's about their application in the reality of the workplace. Thus, the book has to face up to the hard-nosedness implied by the word *management* and speak to the pragmatic realists of the world. The very substance of business is, after all, making products, putting them on the market, and making a profit from them. (The book also has to help us keep in mind that that's not all there is to it.)

To get closer to that practical tough-mindedness, let's call on a group of tough-talking managers. I call them collectively Handy Panel. (Actually it's a composite of many discussions I've had and heard over the years, slanted to get to core issues rather than presented as a "balanced" picture.)

I've asked the panel members for the straight scoop, the real lowdown on integrity and morality in their lives as executives—to "tell it like it is." They leap to the task. Here are their responses:

> "Management is live or die! It's warfare! Hey, we live in the jungle. This isn't a day at the beach! Business is bottom line, baby, and that's all! It's cheat a little even. It means gaining the competitive advantage—and that means advantage *over* somebody else, doesn't it? Maybe you don't like it, but that's reality!"

> "Hey look, we're in a competitive world. You want genteel? Go for tea! Here it's win-lose. Maybe within the company, there's a little win-win; but mostly it's eat or be eaten, beat or be beaten. You don't just sit there and say, 'Hit me again.' It's profits or die, and who wants to be carried out feet first?"

> "It's grow or else! It's grab your share and then some, and don't let anybody grab yours. Managing is hardball, not patty cake–patty cake!"

> "Management simply isn't about cooperating, it's about competing. Oh sure, there's a veneer of politeness, but it's paper thin. You play for keeps. You sweat it. And it gets to you after a while, especially nowadays, with all the interest in business ethics. In the trenches where we play, you keep your back to the wall or someone gets you from behind."

"Hey, it's rough and tumble! You gotta be strong. Yeah, you've got to be tough. Business isn't softness, it's muscle and sinew! Fat, flabby? Forget it! Being a manager is hurrying, it's huffing and puffing; it's not sitting and contemplating your navel."

"You've gotta expand, always expand. Growing is living; standing still is dying. If you're not getting bigger, you're shrinking—it's like you're decaying, pretty soon you go under."

"Good management is *action!* It's movement! Management is a bugle charge up a hill, not a hymn-sing in a church."

"If management were a river, it would be the Mississippi— big, muddy, powerful, and commercial! This isn't some bubbling brook . . . and forget Walden Pond."

"Managing is a doer attitude. It's 'Go,' not 'Whoa!' It's not fiddling around with blueprints and plans; it's rolling up your sleeves and actually building the darned thing, whatever the thing is!"

"You make sure you're the hero, not the goat. You've gotta be a tiger, not a sheep! You can't cower. In business you don't go for mediocrity; you go for greatness. It's passion. It's aggressiveness! It's not sitting on the bench watching the game. It's being out there on the field with the taste of blood in your mouth and the smell of churned-up grass. It's playing hard and playing to win."

Many people say, "Yeah, that gusto game is for me, too!" Isn't that what we're all in it for—the aliveness, the spice in it?

BUT WHERE'S THE SPIRIT?

Despite the panel's brave words, there are some discords in their song. Sorry, panel, it's not that I totally disbelieve you, but as I and many others like me roam the rooms of management we hear as many bleats as roars— maybe more—and meet as many sheep as lions.

There's a smoothness, a smothered vitality, and a lack of integrity in management these days that's different from the way we like to fantasize it. Are the panel's answers make-believe? Has the battle been supplanted by something more hushed? Where's the roar? Where did the guts go? Where's the spirit?

Part of that flatness has to do with lack of truth. That win-or-else bravado in the panel's remarks is mostly fantasy, and we all know it. Nevertheless, life without that gamey stuff seems lacking, so we perpetuate it. Better, now, to replace it with thoughts more suited to these times.

THE NEW GAME

The new game has already begun and it's as rugged as ever. Today's managers have to play better (not just tougher) to win this one—and they've got much to achieve with very little time left on the clock. It's not just reshaping the old, it's respiriting it—reinspiring—which literally means to take in new breath. It's drawing on a new life force. It's utilizing new kinds of power—character power, for example.

The new game is to find the clues to the mystery of human restlessness. We have to locate the long-lost portal to peace of mind and enter that door again. We need to cross over into the vastness of our inner worlds, rediscover and move back into lost parts of ourselves, as though we're clearing cobwebs out of an almost-forgotten upstairs room to make it habitable again.

So let's shelve the tough talking for a while. The new game is like going home, with all that home entails: a warm hearth, a light left on for us, feeling understood, and being able to just *do* life without sweating it so much. The new game is the game that we have, at some level, longed to play all our lives: being able to set aside fear and live a life of more integrity. If we only come close to doing that, it will be worth the journey.

A final introductory word about our "capacity" to embrace important new messages. Let's illustrate it first:

> Three young women, longtime followers of Sai Baba, go to him in India, asking him to heal their friend back in Montana of her cancer. He listens earnestly, looks off in the distance a moment as though resigned to something, and quietly asks, "But where is the capacity?"

This idea of capacity, although a bit new here, comes up in several places later and grows crisper. For now, "capacity" refers to the open-armed attitude we need as we delve into something that's different. In the state of increased capacity we can travel to those places within where fresh messages are received.

PART I

RESPIRITING

REAWAKENING TO SPIRIT IN MANAGEMENT AND LIFE

This part grounds spirit in an explanation of what it is; how it fits into the new management agenda; how it relates to, and yet differs from, energy; and how important it is for us to live in a state of *constant spiritual awareness*. The point: we *can*, and must, go home again.

CHAPTER 1

THE NEW MANAGEMENT AGENDA

> *Most of us have jobs that are too
> small for our spirits.*
> —Studs Terkel

> *Each man is haunted until his
> humanity awakens.*
> —William Blake

The key questions for today's managers and leaders are no longer issues of task and structure but are questions of spirit. When you point this out— *pling!*—some inner chord resonates. People come awake. They lean forward; heads nod agreement, shoulders square up, eyes become more alert, more serious, more hopeful. There's truth here.

Let's repeat it: the key issues facing today's manager-leaders are no longer of task and structure; they're questions of spirit! People know that, and you know they know. It flashes in their body language, their "vibes," even if they've never thought about it this way.

It's signaling there's a new management agenda these days. The usual issues of productivity, organization, finances, costs, profits, and so forth are of course still with us—and will remain as critical as ever. And remaining with us also will be our concerns about the humanness and health of the organization, including things like culture, communications, relationships, and morale.

But those flashes of body language when people hear of an agenda with spirit in it signal something even beyond all that. It's people's spirit voicing truth. "Good!" it's saying. "Let's get around to the real issues of

11

life. Let's get to purpose and meaning, and further, to feelings of emptiness and to our true experience of life itself.

"Let's get to whether care and respect for others in work really pays off. Let's look at how much I truly believe in my work—and how I can begin to believe again. Let's face up to the basic values of my organization—and how a person can live a truer life in a system that doesn't support basic honesty. And let's grab hold of the real issues in managing and leading responsibly in times like these!"

Bringing all this down to earth—to the page—is our task here. So let's picture a management model (below) that consists of four overlapping, interdependent agendas, one of which—the new one—is Spirit. Imagine an expanded pretzel—four rings instead of three—and you've got it.

Each ring symbolizes an agenda for managers: upper left, the head agenda (intellectual); upper right, the heart agenda (feelings); lower left, the body agenda (wellness); and lower right, the new one, the Spirit agenda. Get the picture? Technically, it may be a Venn diagram, but superpretzels are tastier. Although our appetite is for the fresh new segment, let's first sample the other three.

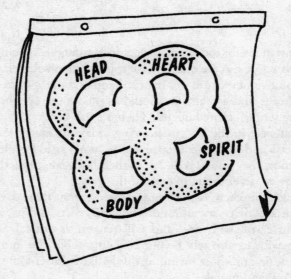

THE HEAD

This is the intellectual curriculum, the upper-left loop—the left brain of organizational management. This is the linear thinking and logic ring, where people walk around with charts and trends and graphs and curves. This agenda attends to the issues of shaping and running the organization, of breaking down tasks so they get done most efficiently. This head agenda has to do with how it's all structured so that it works. It's very practical and necessary.

We think of this as the intellectual foundation upon which the enterprise is built. During the formative years of modern management this was the docket that consumed managers' time and attention. They thought about it, studied it, worried about it, brought it home, and dreamt of it. This was the early make-or-break agenda. And this is our gene pool. These same questions occupy today's managers with as much intensity as ever. We can now better understand the current left-brained shape of management.

THE HEART

"But what about the heart, pal?" people asked back then and are still asking. "The problem with the head agenda is that it organizes the work all right, but it leaves out the human beings who do the work!" "You can't hire a hand," Professor Burling at Cornell used to drum into us. You hire the whole person—feelings, human needs, social behavior, and, nowadays, spirit.

The heart agenda is the right brain, the upper-right pretzel loop—the feeling side of management. It brings to the table the legitimacy of emotions and the power of caring; it focuses on issues of human worth, such as dignity, team play, morale, and trust.

There's a perceived tension between the two agendas; to some, it's an epic struggle between hard- and softheadedness. Head agenda: logical, seen as fixated on productivity; heart agenda: psychological, emotional, viewed as soft on production. Each agenda demands the attention of managers, each side counterbalancing the other, each necessary for the whole. We should be grateful for both sides.

THE BODY

Nowadays there's a third agenda: the body agenda concerned about wellness in the workplace. Questions considered here relate to employees' physical health and the collective health of the organizational body. This may be younger and thinner than the other agendas, but it brings the sparkle of health. And it's making inroads. How does such an item compete for time and space on an already-crowded agenda?

As someone said, it takes a lot to get the attention of the fat guys in the boardroom—and lately, people in jogging suits, obviously not board-of-directors types, have been seen leaving the boardroom holding hands with those big guys. Odd couples, indeed. What brings these unlikely sorts together? The body agenda.

Put yourself in the board member's shoes (black wing-tip oxfords). You're sitting in the boardroom. If it's a good board, this is not just a plush room with shiny wooden table in it, it's a problem-slaying chamber. But you've got an ice bag on your head; obviously you've got a big headache. Why? Because for the last several years you've been struggling with a runaway brute problem: employee health care costs have raced from practically zip to 8 percent or even 18 percent or more of payroll! Whew! This, at a time when the company is running for its life. Zillions of unbudgeted bucks, each a dour surprise, and nobody likes surprises!

Suddenly, along comes the possibility of relief. You might be able to cut those costs and recover a chunk of those runaway dollars. Would you care if the person bringing the relief is some tanned health nut wearing leotards? Finding money is nutritious stuff! These odd couples are now conjuring up wellness programs aimed at educating and inspiring the whole work force to improve its health by dieting, exercising, quitting smoking, reducing weight, and cutting back stress.

If a wellness program saves just a few people from heart attacks or gall-stones or ulcers, the return is ample. Just think of the costs—insurance, replacements, training, lost production, and so on—as well as the human loss, and then multiply it all by N (the number in the work force). The figures impress; the boardroom guys perk up, and maybe even thin down a little.

Good health pays off, and the benefit goes further than the bottom line. A healthy work force composed of healthy individuals is a more energetic work force; morale is higher, they produce more, and they feel part of a caring family. It's a way to inject good messages—"You're important, the whole you"—and it's coming at a time when people's spirits are yearning for caring signals from their organizations.

THE SPIRIT

Now, let's look at the Spirit agenda, which consists of ancient issues coming home, mooring at the docket of management. Included in this agenda are cosmic queries. And here, finally, is the curriculum of human-kind's eternal search to be a part of something greater.

This agenda takes us beyond the other three—past the head, the heart, and the body—deep into the inner self. This is the calendar of the soul. It was inevitable that these questions, so prominent in our private lives, would someday spill over into the workplace to touch us all.

Spirit agenda questions aren't easily or simply answered. Some are in fact unanswerable, but they do demand our earnest attention. You've heard them: What is it all about? What is my purpose here (at work, in life)? Who am I? Where is all this leading? Where? To a percentage point more profit next quarter? Is that all? Is that *it?*

Where's it leading me? To greater worldly success? To another promotion? Really? At what cost? Is it leading to more work, to more lonely time too distant from family? To the gold watch at retirement? Or even to a golden parachute? Is life simply a matter of being born, drifting along like a leaf in the stream, doing, doing, doing—and then, worn, wan, and water-soaked, to sink? Is that all? There's got to be more to life than that!

What about happiness? What about contentment, the deepest kind of happiness? And meaning? Is my work a net benefit in this world? Where's this "truth" I keep hearing about? And where's peace—not just world peace, but inner peace—peace in my world, my inner universe?

In England, at the start of a workshop on organizational transformation, we form into small circles to discuss these kinds of questions. The last question on our list is, What is it that I yearn for at a deep level in my life? The group is quiet.

Jan, a shy Dutch businessman, smiles nervously, then stares off into space a moment. It is his turn to lead off with an answer. His eyes return to the circle of friendly faces. He clears his throat, and whispers, "Peace." The immensity of that word hits the group. Jan's throat catches, his eyes brim with tears. Embarrassed, he composes himself, glances quickly at the others, and sees that they're feeling it with him. He grins crookedly, "Isn't that what we all yearn for?"

Yes, that's what we yearn for. We're hungry for purpose and meaning and identity, too. We're hungry for a richer encounter with living; we're starving for the experience of having a full, vibrant "life" while we're here on this planet. We hunger for an understanding of who we are and how we fit into this whole. It's as though the ages without answers have sharpened the hunger. Sooner or later it gnaws at all of us.

WHAT IS SPIRIT?

> *There is a dimension of the uni-*
> *verse unavailable to the senses.*
> —Joseph Campbell

We've talked about it, but what is spirit, really? Simply put, spirit is our nonbody self (or the nonbodily self of an organization). Spirit is that part of us that is

Beyond this physical body (including the brain)

Beyond flesh, blood, bones, and heartbeat

Beyond the need for food and sleep

Beyond the five senses

Beyond mind, thoughts

Beyond feelings

Beyond passions, desires

Beyond memories and innate tendencies

Spirit is the *us* beyond all the things we usually think are the real us. It requires a little flip-flop of our definition of reality.

We all think of ourselves as the body. We just assume this leather bag with nine holes in it is us. And it is, in a way. This body walks, talks, breathes, eats, and feels heat and cold. To some of us, it's a great thing to have around; to others, a cause of concern. But the real question is, *Is* this body the real us?

Wisdom tells us it's not. Ask people to indicate the self. "Here I am," they say, with a hand raised to their chest. Notice they are not pointing to their face. How come? If that's the most recognizable part of us, why not point to it? What are they pointing to? The heart—that muscle-pump behind the sternum? No. They're pointing *inside*. They're gently touching what some call the spiritual heart. Something within is directing: "Here, I'm inside, this is me—spirit."

Is this mere fancy, a poetic interpretation of a common gesture? Some might say so, but who's to say what reality is? Let's watch Aunt Tilly for an answer. When husband Elmer passes away, Tilly sits by him and asks, "Why did you leave me, where have you gone?" But why is she saying that if she's sitting beside him? The answer: she's not really sitting beside him because he's no longer there. The real Elmer left and she knows it.

At life-and-death times in our life, we know what reality is. The real Elmer is the aliveness that once inhabited the body she's seated beside. It was Elmer's body that died; the real Elmer has gone, or returned, somewhere.

Spirit, as used here, refers to our (and our organizations') aliveness, which is the real *us*. Spirit is the vitality that dwells in our body; it's our energy and zest. And spirit refers also to the very source of that energy which is at some level, of course, within us and a part of us. For now, then, spirit refers to our other reality, our real reality, our higher reality—the one which at some inner level we know exists but at times forget that we know.

Waking Up Spirit

Robert, a friend-client, is the new general manager of a cobwebby organization. He has been called in to get the place moving again. The people in the organization are good enough, but they're in trouble. There's a general lack of purpose and a void of spirit in the place.

Imagine a wagon train stalled on the prairie: Studebaker wagons half loaded, mules unhitched, drivers (the management group) sitting and standing around. They know they should be rolling out but can't get it together enough to move. They seem to be waiting for someone to shout, "Head 'em up!"; but they've ignored the yells of eager young general managers before.

Robert himself is going through a similar "stuckness." For years he has striven for the top job. Now he's got it—and he's in anticlimactic shock. Is this all there is? I mean, this is *It*? His own spiritual malaise in a way mirrors the company's dilemma, and it brings a certain integrity to the whole effort. It's now beyond simply a management technique or strategy problem. Robert's personal life inquiry dovetails the organization's.

The organization embarks on a respiriting program, with an attitude of widespread involvement driving the program. The emphasis is on the question, What's our grand purpose?

Questions drawn from the Spirit agenda are struggled with: Who are we? What are we really doing here? What is our purpose, our calling, our vision of greatness? What is the something bigger than us that we're a part of here?

The result is a new credo for the organization that details how they will operate. Central to it is the theme of continuous involvement, not only of employees but also of suppliers and customers.

Eventually their efforts bring a self-fueling energy to the place. It's not easy. They bump along the improvement trail for over a year; and by the end of it, there's much more intensity in the company atmosphere and they're becoming more accustomed to moving and accomplishing.

Meanwhile Robert's interest in spirit in the workplace and within himself continues. He reads, thinks, talks, and ponders. Months later I receive a letter from him summarizing some of his ruminating. This is part of that letter:

I see "vision" as a spiritual phenomenon because it goes beyond everyday issues . . . . Vision is a spiritual way to create organizational bonding without the use of coercion.

One of the hardest things I have come to realize as a general manager is that my state of mind is really my primary tool . . . . My everyday life is spent dispersing energy, and keeping a mental focus is a full-time effort.

I need time every day to develop vision and focus. I suppose a daily dose of meditation, which is not my current routine, would be helpful to remind myself daily of the spiritual side.

Being a highly rational, task-oriented doer in a busy management job is not directly compatible with understanding and practicing spirituality. There's a continual need for calming so that spiritual wisdom can come through.

He finished with a line from a Sufi poem: "when I am quiet and solid as the ground, then I talk the low tones of thunder for all."

CHAPTER 2

CONSTANT SPIRITUAL AWARENESS

One of the key ideas in this book is that we can, and need to, be both spirit and body—concurrently. That, in a sense, is the whole point. We need to change our mind in a literal sense; we need to develop an expanded consciousness—no less than that—an awareness that includes spirit. Always.

A couple of years ago, Louise and I were in England working our way toward India. We were to give a presentation at a management colloquy near London, and we had some time before and after to rest and prepare. I expected to use the days before the conference to allow my internal time zone to move closer to Greenwich mean time and to get myself into a mental place for our session. Looking for a way to achieve this peace but not knowing quite where to go, I felt as if our rental car took over; we wandered toward the southwest, finally choosing Glastonbury for what we hoped would be a rejuvenating few days.

On the surface Glastonbury is one of those pretty little English villages where the people are polite and the food is blah. But this little village is more than a pretty place in nature, it is also a lovely state of mind. Legend and history intermingle mysteriously here until you're not sure which is which and it doesn't matter. Its history as a spiritual place stretches back countless centuries, millennia before history even, earlier than we can imagine. It is said that this is the location of the mystical Isle of Avalon of the King Arthur legends. But even before Arthur and his knights sat at the round table, Saint Patrick stopped here to form an order of monks. And even before that, long before people started recording history, signs hint that this was a hub of ceremony and mystery.

Consequently it is a wondrous place for us to rest and prepare ourselves. We enjoy daily doses of enchantment—walking the ancient Abbey grounds, quiet contemplation on the Tor, which is a steep little hill on the edge of town that almost puts you in sight of ancient Avalon and the ages of yore.

On our last morning we visit the Chalice Well, an artesian spring, which for thousands of years has been pouring an undiminished flow of cool drink—an everlasting gift for those who journey here. I spend time alone at the lower garden pool which is fed by the well up the rise. I'm seated in the warming morning sun, breathing the clean air, enjoying the softness of the place, the insects buzzing, butterflies dancing in the sunlight. I contemplate this fountainhead, this source of eternally flowing sweetness. As I sit there, I'm experiencing one of those special intervals of neither plan nor schedule, a nothing-to-do time when one is more open to the gifts of the universe.

I'm at peace. My mind is not directly on the coming conference presentation, but somewhere, inside, I suppose I'm mulling over how to communicate these airy ideas to the concrete business types at the conference.

After a while I wander a few score yards up the flowered path to the well itself. At first, it appears to be an ordinary round well extending slightly above ground level. And then, it comes alive . . .

On the well opening is a wooden hatch cover, perhaps four feet in diameter, and on the face of it is a decorative emblem in black metal. Like a giant disk hurled by the gods, it flies up off the hatch cover and enters my awareness. Here is the graphic symbol for my presentation!

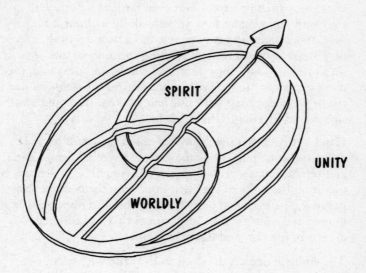

The emblem consists of two overlapping circles, one above the other, both within a larger circle. Pointing up through it all is an arrow, its notch at the bottom of the ring, its point at the top.

The universe has sent me a picture worth a thousand words, a visual symbol that reveals three powerful ideas:

Our everyday, or "worldly," self (lower self)

Spirit, or our higher self

The two interconnected, united as one

This symbol portrays to me the two realities—the spiritual and the worldly—and shows that they coexist as a unified whole, always in touch, overlapping. It also shows spirit coexisting with the body: both always there, together; *both* necessary for completeness; wholeness impossible if either isn't there.

Without both, it's like listening to a stereo recording with the knob turned to mono. Remember how rich it sounds after you switch to stereo? Not even noticed before, yet afterward you wonder how you got along without it for so long. No wonder so many people feel a vacancy in their lives: they aren't aware of their indwelling spirit, so in that sense it isn't present. Thus, they don't feel whole; and unwhole, they don't experience integrity. It's like wearing a patch over one eye or wearing glasses with one lens broken. It's living a half-sighted, half-feelinged, half-rich life.

I find out later that the symbol is called the *vesica piscis*. It serves the same purpose as the yin/yang symbol from China and similar images from antiquity. The emblem is a means of picturing the unity of apparent opposites: the positive and negative, the male and female, the visible and invisible, the known and unknowable. It illustrates that two different aspects of life can, and do, exist as one.

The emblem depicts the deep truth that reality is not two separate forces but is one. It pictures *Unity!* The ancients knew deep unity, a truth that is immortalized on the well cover. But we forget this deep truth because we're programmed to an either-or world. We forget that both (and even that all) is one. It makes such clear sense to me that I'm sure the concrete types at the business conference will get it.

Thus prepared, I approach my colloquy talk. I title it "Constant Spiritual Awareness" and I talk of the need to be in unity with one's spirit even while fully operating in the day-to-day "real" world. I help explain it with this simple symbol: circles within a circle.

The lower circle represents our bodily, or worldly, self—the nonspiritual world of matter. This is the self who is the performer we live with every day. It's our supposed real self, the visible self who exists in the natural world. If we pinch it, this self feels something. We often think that this is our only self.

When we think that way, we get caught up in the body and live that half-complete life mentioned earlier. We worry about the body, pamper it, cater to its senses; stuff it with food one minute and sweat off excess weight the next; powder it, please it, protect it.

Yet at some level we know that life in this body is but a three-day fair. We're well aware of our mortality; nevertheless, we act as though this body will last forever, and we pay scant regard to our spirit. Thus, we're trapped in that lower circle, half-sized, feeling incomplete.

The upper circle denotes our higher self—the reality beyond the pull of body and senses. It's the self we "know" is there but don't know that we know. The higher circle is spirit, which has been lost to us, causing the hunger we all feel for purpose, meaning, and richness of life. It's the self Walt Whitman sings of as "the other I" in *Leaves of Grass.*

I weave into my presentation psychologist Roberto Assagioli's (1971) point that the central drama of humankind is the fusion of one's personality with one's higher self. Whether humans aspire to this goal consciously or unconsciously, or are pushed toward it by their inability to find true peace of mind, this (upward arrow) is the direction of the flow. And now we're coming home—our generation, apparently the fortunate ones, readying to become whole, as spirit revives in our time.

Then, I read some lines from Juan Ramon Jiménez's poem, as translated by Robert Bly (1990):

> I am not I.
>
>   I am this one
> Walking beside me, whom I do not see,
> Whom at times I manage to visit,
> And at other times I forget.
> . . . .
> The one who remains silent when I talk,
> . . . .
> The one who will remain standing when I die.

Finally, I speak of the American Indian ideal of actually living one's life in a state of constant spiritual awareness. For Native Americans the ideal mode of everyday life is to work, drive the roads, listen to the radio, hunt, fish, watch the news, go to school, relate to family—whatever—and always be in spirit. It's similar to the Taoist or Buddhist affirmation of the physical "stream of events" that flows over our worldly self as we exist in life. The Indian ideal is to create an existence in which there is absolutely no difference between the physical and spiritual worlds. None! Always, at *every* moment, ever in a state of completeness—missing nothing.

The audience is quiet. Heads are nodding ardent agreement but they're not speaking; they're just taking it in. After the presentation, one man, a business consultant from Sweden, lingers. He's ready to melt. Chin quivering, eyes filled, he reaches to touch me, thanks us (Louise and me), and tells us how the idea of constant spiritual awareness has helped him see that his life can be more complete. After a minute or two he says he needs to stay behind alone in the room for a while. We tell him we'll leave our spirits with him and take our bodies to the lounge. He laughs.

Later, smiling and obviously lighter, he buys me a drink and further explains how the presentation and picture touched him deeply with the possibility of recovering this long-lost aspect of himself. I can see the importance of this to him and feel good about it. He does, too.

Constant spiritual awareness, as we said, is nothing less than a new state of mind for most people. It's a fresh way of being, a more complete way of life, one that helps bring back the wholeness they yearn for. That's the central idea of the new management agenda.

> Spirit is with us all the time, including the time, a couple of years ago, when I found myself standing with a guy from IBM on a sand dune overlooking the Sea of Cortez. (This was before Big Blue's restructuring blues of the early nineties.) It was early morning. We had just met. He had the conservative mien of an IBM middle manager, but for now we were a couple of unshaven gringos about two hundred kilometers down the Baja peninsula in Mexico. Vagabonds for a few weeks, we were meandering our separate ways, going slowly southward.

> We were enjoying the freedom and beauty of it all. The day was a typical Baja day: warm winter sun, yellow-tan sand meeting blue sky at the horizon, with the same blue in the sea, pelicans skimming a few inches above the waves. The soft surf sounds and the morning zephyrs were exerting good influences below the level of awareness.

> He had parked up the beach and that morning had invited me for a mug of coffee. We chatted idly about nothing in particular. After a while the subject turned to the vaunted

service ethic of his company. He talked about how the company budgeted and staffed its service organization. The more he explained, and saw that my interest was sincere, the more alive our conversation became.

The surroundings, the atmosphere, the perspective you get when so far away with no ax to grind, when you can just be there at that moment, able to simply be humans—it all helped bring home the truth and importance in what he was saying.

"Regardless of how other products may compare to ours," he said, "it's our service—it's the spirit of service in all of us that makes us what we are." His eyes shone with this feeling and his voice caught a bit. I acted as though I didn't notice. "Our service," he gathered himself and continued, "just will not be beaten." There was no arrogance or conceit in what he said, no self-importance—only pride, the warm, happy kind. He was proud and pleased he could say such a thing.

What made him feel that way was nothing material, not a product; it wasn't bodily or worldly. It was something intangible, yet very, very real and wonderfully powerful! Being a part of that company ethic—a part of that spirit— living those high-minded ideals made him a bigger, more noble person.

We both went our separate ways. But that encounter in the wilderness in Mexico stays with me. At that time the conven- tions of the *vagabundos* brotherhood didn't allow me to reach for his hand, shake it, and say, "Thanks for revealing some of your company's spirit, for showing me something so personal and important—and so universal." I wish now that I had.

MOVING TOWARD SPIRIT

When people seek to "motivate" the work force or put "life" back into their lives, they're searching for the fountain of vitality. They're looking for the lost sparkle, foraging for vanished vim, vigor, and verve—for the spirit that comes from Source. As we draw nearer to that Source, that causal force, our existence takes on heartiness. We're closer to our essence, to that which makes us alive.

Professor Peter Vaill (1989), who has observed successful organizations for over a decade, says that case studies and other research results that have come out about high-performing systems consistently refer to the "spirit" people feel. The "spiritual dimension," as he puts it, is always involved in situations of great achievement. This is what accounts for the special energy—the inspiration, enthusiasm, vigor, and so forth—that you find in these high-achievement environments.

Vaill (1989) also refers to consultant-author Tom Peters's (1987) comment that the quality improvement programs that really work are "almost mystical." It's an excellent point, but not quite strong enough. The programs that really work, the ones that give birth to major change, *are* mystical (*mystical* is defined here as having the remarkable power to insinuate the program's values into every soul in the organization and into everything these beings think and do). You can almost taste the inner meaning and importance of these programs. It may not be noisy (it may be rather quiet even), but it's as if you can't not go along with them.

> It's several years ago. We're working on a productivity improvement program that takes on these insinuative powers. The effort initially includes all seventy-nine of the organization's first-level managers. This is the level just above supervisors. Later, the program spreads to supervisors and the whole work force.
>
> Over the years the manager-level people grew a thick hide in order to resist the usual kicking and spurring by top management when productivity fell. We are asked in at this point because one of the executives senses that going to the whip again simply won't work.
>
> This time the top brass choose to listen to people instead of cracking the whip. After the inevitable sparring, as the managers test top management's sincerity, the brass learns to join, honestly, *with* the managers in the process of wrestling productivity out of the situation. Finally, managers are being listened to, after years, or even whole careers, of pretending to work together; this recognition brings the levels of management closer together.
>
> Slowly rapport builds—and with that, a great feeling of accord

(let's say it's mystical) comes and touches the program. Everyone—managers, and eventually supervisors and workers—gets behind it like never before. Upper management listens, while lower management, and ultimately the whole work force, feels heard. They all arrive at a deeper appreciation of the others and begin to share in the hard, competitive truth of their circumstances.

When people come to appreciate truth, it's the same as coming to spirit. That's the source of the great energy in this program. Spirit is what brings the *mystical* quality. People are drawn to the effort and charge it with an almost irresistible power that makes it work. Productivity and quality soar over 30 percent the first year, and the improvements continue in subsequent years despite even greater pressures to produce.

But, to be honest, productivity isn't the real profit from this situation. Sure, everyone can point to the figures and be proud; but the real power, the magic in it, is the new *spirit* in the company. It infuses every participant with something special. People walk a little taller during the years of the program. There is more *life* in them.

Chuckie, an old friend, is the opposite of aliveness when he drags by my office one day. Shoulders hunched, chin on the ground, his heart isn't in our agenda. After a while it comes out: his puppy was run over by a car that morning. A cute, warm, loving, earth-colored dog—now gone.

We drift into contemplating life and death. Where did that life force go? we wonder. Where did the spirit that animated the animal drift off to? It was there a while ago. Raw energy. Now nothing. Worse than nothing. The body is there, but now it's only matter—just chemistry. Inert.

When the dog was born, some mysterious force touched that inert matter and turned it into a life! That "force" is Spirit bringing energy (we get more into that subject in chapter 3). Life—created just like *that!* An alchemic pat and—*pop!*—it's a pup, a panting, slurping, little brown pooch. Then, as quickly as it was given, it is taken. That force from Source comes and goes. Without that invisible force, the pup is just stuff again. Without that life force, life isn't.

Chuckie and I eventually get around to our original agenda. The real learning for us that day, however, and the only memories still alive are our musings about life, vitality, and puppies.

I guess it's impossible to contemplate this spirit-essence which is life without also considering it's counterpart.

In India, neighbor Al is very ill. Yellow, extremely thin, skin erupting, he has been this way for six or eight weeks. There is some malevolence in his liver. We talk about death and how it is never far away. We talk about the cremations at the river a half-kilometer distant. "Too much rain this year, the water level is too high," I tell him, wanting to switch the focus back to the living. "Wait till next year to go."

Death—the ultimate unfastener—is always close by. Here, in India, it feels even nearer, like a small pressure nudging you along, reminding you of the inevitable. It's part of the gift of India. The awareness of death's imminence is also an awareness of life's wondrous presence.

Al knows this. It's interesting, his struggle with, and final acceptance of, the ultimate question of life and death. As he founders physically, his energy actually seems to move from his thin body to expand outward in all directions, into Spirit. And that alters his energy.

A calm happiness, an ecstasy, settles around him even in the face of his grinding illness. Tartness turns into sweetness. Smiles flash easily across the wan face. His acceptance brings fearlessness—and with that, a welcoming of these life circumstances. It's the ultimate human capacity, the supreme act of accepting and embracing.

Al knows that he, the bodily he, is not the final phase of his being. This "knowing" doesn't stem from logic; it's more of a cosmic allowing which transpires at a level beyond thought.

He has come to know and befriend the Reaper, which then,
of course, loses its awful power.

A similar process occurs with terminally ill patients. Facing death, which
is the absolute end of their worldly self, people move into Spirit and don't
worry about the worldly stuff anymore. And aren't we all under the same
sentence? Isn't dying without fear, in a state of peace, one of the aims of the
big game, life?

SO WHY BOTHER?

Need the rationale for all this? It's a reasonable request. Why should we (we
personally, as well as "we" our organizations) bother with this constant
spiritual awareness? Here are three reasons: (1) to get in step with oneself,
(2) to bring health, and (3) to attune to life's purpose.

Getting In Step with Oneself

Our move toward spirit is inevitable. Some do it more consciously than
others, but all seem to do it one way or another during their lifetime. And
nowadays, more and more people, including those in business leadership
positions, are at some level conscious of this general movement toward
spirit.

"In step" doesn't necessarily mean we conform with the world, but
the increasing spiritual awareness afoot in the land can serve as a clue to
those who are hungering for something more. Where's my spirit? is the
question. Full or empty?

Friend Tom, a management consultant, calls and says, "I've noticed
I'm getting a deeper kind of question lately. After trust builds, clients get
down to the profoundly perplexing question of whether what they're doing
really has meaning in this world. That's a spiritual question, Jack." The
next day Bob, another old friend, also a consultant, calls with essentially the
same observation: "Clients everywhere are questioning the big house and
the boat; they're asking deep, almost spiritual questions, Jack." "You bet,"
is my retort to both.

When asked to name their heroes in a *Fortune* magazine survey
(which we mentioned in the introduction), rich Americans (those with six-
figure incomes) listed Mother Teresa most often. "Mother Teresa!" laughs
Mike, my business professor friend, as he inserts a mental asterisk in his
warehouse of management knowledge. Yes, Mother Teresa—and she's
mentioned along with Einstein, huge business hero (at that time) Lee

Iacocca, and that ilk. What's showing through here? It's the higher selves of the business readers who answered the survey; it's their own innate and inevitable leaning toward spirit.

Here's another brief illustration (also touched on in the introduction): at an exclusive dinner party in Newport Beach for the Dalai Lama when he won the Nobel Peace Prize, the most often asked question by the lions of industry who were there was, How can we introduce more ethics and spirituality into our businesses and everyday lives? The answer from His Holiness was gentle and interesting ("Do it from the heart, within your own culture"), but it is the repeated question that really grabs our attention here. These superexecutives' interest in this subject reflects and presages the widespread, probably unavoidable turn toward spirit that's occurring in all walks of life.

Bringing Health

We become healthier as we move closer to spirit. Health, in the business world, means we and our organizations are stronger, happier, more focused, better able to compete, more likely to play a good game—and will probably come up winning more often.

Call it high performance if you like. Whatever it is, people who examine this form of healthiness invariably begin talking about spirit— the spirit in the organization and in the people involved.

Attunement with Life's Purpose

Finally, we need to bother with all this simply because, whether or not we know it, that's our real goal in life. Period. It's that simple.

Why are we here? We're here to experience fully this life, this brio, this force that was infused into this particular bodily matter. We may not know what our mission is while we're here, or even whether we have one, but we do know in the deepest core of our existence that we have some spiritual values that we're compelled to satisfy. We know that we must live this life fully. Better yet, we know full well when we're *not* living life fully. Does this mean we should make a go-for-the-gusto grab at a life? No. It means, simply, that we have to attune to the inevitable and move toward those deepest-held values, toward higher self, closer to Source.

Relate this to business organizations: it means we need to move closer to the grand purposes of the firm, the fundamental, the larger-than-life reasons why we do what we do.

It's simply right for us to do it, to be congruent with higher self this way. Those internal signals are our best indicators that this is the right way for us. When we don't pay attention to this, we feel the emptiness and lack of fulfillment that so many speak of; when we do, we simply feel better. The big aim is to become whole, to realize our full Self—both circles, higher and lower, Spirit and worldly.

That's what it's all about. Our life direction, if you will, is to move into the vacant upstairs flat and become *constant spiritual awareness.* That's the *why* of life—to live a life well lived, a life of real satisfaction and peace—closer to home.

Chapter 3

Working with Energy and Spirit

Am I the bulb or the light?
—Joseph Campbell

Spirit is something you get into;
energy is what you get from that.
—J. H.

Moving toward higher self creates energy, and energy—organizational or personal—is strength. Moving upward brings vigor. As we tap Source, life force flows to meet us. This is appealing if you're out there sweating, facing the challenges of life, fighting the battle, playing the game, doing your best. And who isn't?

SORTING FORCE FROM SOURCE

Notice that I use the words *energy* and *Spirit* separately. They are so close we can often use the terms interchangeably. At times, however, we've got to be more precise. Spirit, big-*S* Spirit, is the solid core, the stable, unchanging foundation. It is Source. It is the whence, whence all else comes. Energy, on the other hand, is power and dynamism, intensity and motion.

If we were to enter into the phenomenon of Spirit and magically picture how it works, I imagine we would find a solid rock labeled "Spirit," with some squiggly lines emanating from it that reach out and touch things in the world. These lines are the energy, the current, the juice, the connections that bring about the phenomenal results we attribute to Spirit. But they aren't Spirit, they're just the force of it.

Energy (and all the words for it, such as *vitality, gusto, zest,* and even the word *spirit*—little-*s spirit*) is the action component, the movement, the dance. It is the invisible pull or push we feel. We often act upon energy to change it—focus it, increase it, release it, and redirect it—but energy is not Spirit, it's not Source.

Releasing Spirit can bring an avalanche of energy and zest. Suddenly, we have more strength, more vim for facing life's challenges.

It's worth repeating: when we broach Spirit, we emancipate energy; we reactivate the cache of enthusiasm that lives inside. It may not have the sudden, energy-bringing *toot! toot!* of Popeye's tin of spinach, but it comes! It's a method of turning up the juice in order to effect heartiness in our personal and organizational lives.

As I'm working on these spirit and energy chapters in India, a curious and, it turns out, instructive thing happens: alien invaders suddenly come and wrench away all my energy. Hmmm. I awaken one morning feeling tired and vaguely nauseous. I don't pay attention to it as stomach sickness is a way of life here—always lurking, ready to grab. I've been grabbed and yanked by it before, but this time it overwhelms.

Chills. Fever. Cramps. Diarrhea. Vomiting. The microbe legion attacks on all fronts. The onslaught is swift and vicious. During the next three hours I have five increasingly gut-wrenching attacks. As I said, these attacks happen, but every once in a while you hear of one that hits with such force that it's a killer.

Babu's brother, the taxi driver, helps carry me down the three flights of stairs and then takes me to the little hospital. They put me in bed and stick an IV into me. They also inject me with something to stop the vomiting.

My temperature spikes at 106 degrees Fahrenheit (41 degrees Celsius). Waves of deliria flow through me. Even then, I'm distantly aware of these chapters and make mental notes about what happens when energy flees. I can't even walk, talk, or look at anything. I can't smell anything (probably a good thing). At times I can't hear anybody. Just a few hours ago I was my vigorous self, now I'm close to inert.

Inside, my delirium is a screechy, indecipherable babble. Loud, demanding voices are screaming questions at me from all directions. The questions and voices seem to be brawling for space in my head. It's a wild, tense jumble of sounds and feelings—a fracas, an inquisition. It's all related, I sense, to these chapters.

I notice that the screamed-out questions are put in such a way that the answers must be no. This makes it even worse because the continual noes create a negative mood which brings the wrong energy for a time like this. Nevertheless, I'm beset by squawking demands for no—over and over, wrenched out of me: "No . . . no . . . no . . ."

As soon as I give one no, another, deeper interrogation is angrily flung at me: "Is this what you wanna say? No? Then is *this* the way you wanna say it? *No!*? Hrrumph, then is *THIS?*" But that characterization is far too mild; it's more frenzied and savage than that. In my febrile craziness many voices are screeching more complicated questions. They're hurling them at me all at once, shouting, elbowing, insisting. I have no power here against this angry, merciless interrogation; I'm trapped. I can't not answer . . .

In a semilucid interval, an image that I had while meditating two years ago drifts back to me. I lightly called it a "cosmic vision" then. It was a large, spiral, watch-spring-like shape, consisting of many coils winding their way toward the center. I followed the coils, around and around, circling deeper and deeper, until I attained the center.

And there, where the spiral motif came in upon itself, was a small, polished, gold pin, needlelike, perhaps two or three centimeters long. It was shiny to the point of glowing, as though it possessed its own source of light. Also existing there were the words: *yes, yes, yes.* They weren't inscribed on the pin; they were simply there in that center, more an idea than a sound. I didn't know then what the experience meant, yet it fascinated me, and I somehow knew it was of great value . . . and now it returns.

As I slip back into my stormy delirium, I bring a plan with me. It's a desperate, feeble, crazy-sounding plan, but I have naught else. The *yes, yes, yes* from the center of that vision might work against the "no" energy draining life from me. There's no logic to it: how can you answer yes to questions demanding no? But I desperately need rest from the cacophony within; my faith in that cosmic spiral is all I have.

I begin, in that wildness, repeating a sound: *Aumsairam* (a Sanskrit phrase that many use to help them turn inward toward a center). I follow each repetition with yes. I begin, weakly, hesitant at first, because the answer seems so exactly wrong. And yet it's my only hope: *Aumsairam*, yes.

"*Aumsairam*, yes," repeated silently, defiantly in the face of the no questions assailing me. "*Aumsairam*, yes. *Aumsairam*, yes" . . . Slowly, slowly, the storm settles. I can sense progress, tiny but timely, against the relentless attack. Louise, who is sitting on the next bed quietly saying some prayers, notices a sort of blanket of peacefulness descending over both of us. She knows then that things will be okay.

As the yesses sound, I begin to writhe less. The IV tube in my arm now seems less like a nail holding me to the hard bed and I'm able to roll slightly on my side and be a bit more comfortable. With that speck of comfort comes relief. Ah, rest. At first, it's a few fitful moments of calm; then, they begin to drift together, fusing into intervals of sorely needed sleep. The fire recedes. Peace descends on this war-torn body.

It's just two days later. I'm tender, yet well enough to be out walking in the cool, early morning. There's some wobble in my gait, and some wobbliness inside, too. I feel humble, subdued. I'm still flabbergasted by the quickness with which my energy was yanked from me; one minute vigorous, the next, vigorless. I reflect on the experience with awe and jot down the following learnings.

THE LEARNINGS COME

Even trying to recall what vigor was like is almost too much exertion. Trying to imagine energy requires thinking. Thinking requires energy, and the cupboard's bare. Thus, you just lie there. It's a sobering, humbling, circular trap. Without physical energy you really are nothing in this worldly world. That pat of life-bringing energy that Chuckie and I talked of earlier becomes clearer to me. When your energy gauge reads empty, it's hard to even imagine how to refill the tank.

In an organizational context you see this also. If the organization receives a great setback of some kind—a huge financial loss, for example, or loss of a big contract bid or customer—it too gets sick; it too suffers a great loss of energy. And it too quantum staggers backward, becoming withdrawn, lethargic, and timid. It too loses its confidence. Without energy, how can it be otherwise?

The task, then, whether individual or organizational, is to revitalize. But how? "You use energy to change energy," says consultant Harrison Owen (1984). He points to the cyclotron as an example: it uses subatomic particles (bits of energy) to bombard other subatomic particles, and the collisions bring about changes in them.

But how does that work with an individual or an organization? Well, the organization's leaders have to eventually find some way to generate or import energy. They find a new source to plug into: a stirring new vision may do it, or new overarching goals that mobilize people, or a new basic meaning that pulls at people's hearts. Or the leaders themselves are changed. New leaders with new energy and fresh viewpoints are brought in, giving the organization a shot of vim.

The zest-recovery example in chapter 1 (Robert, the new general manager who inherited the sleepy organization) is an instance where both strategies were used. First, the new leader was brought in, but that wasn't enough. He had to engage the managers and work force in the reawakening of energy (of Spirit). He did that by involving them in the search for their grand purpose.

Might the concept of using energy to bring back energy fit my illness experience? Let's see. First, Babu's brother's energy conveyed my energy-less body to the care unit. The doctors used their thought energy for diagnosis (thought is a subtle form of energy). A powerful antivomiting energy was injected to counteract the spasm energy. It worked. Then a vein was opened and an energy-bringing solution dripped directly into my bloodstream. That helped too. The cold energy of an ice bag was used against the searing heat of my forehead. It felt good, and feeling good is also a subtle form of energy.

And finally, the yes, yes, yesses. They certainly were a key force in this. Were the yesses a form of sound energy, one sound balancing another? Was it positive thinking overcoming negative? We know there's power in good thoughts. Or perhaps it's more romantic: maybe it's the energy of good overwhelming bad, the forces of dharma, the raw might of right action crushing the evil legions of *adharma!*

Was this an example of energy working on energy? Or was it something more profound, such as Spirit working on spirit? Was it a cosmic hand reaching out to help? Isn't it true that Spirit comes at death times in our lives? Was this one? It didn't feel like it, but who knows what death feels like? And where did the spiral vision come from in the first place? And why did it come back two years later at such an opportune moment?

Perhaps this experience was just a vivid demonstration of energy and Spirit, staged so we learn. Staged? By whom or what? By some inner power? Was I merely acting a role in a teaching drama? Could that be what life is?

Or could it even be that this is a peek beyond energy, a deep tap into Spirit? Maybe the watch-spring vision symbolizes the wellspring of energy, while the "yes" mantra is the energy emanating from that, as if the rock-and-wavy-lines principle (discussed at the beginning of this chapter) were being acted out before our very eyes.

MANAGING ENERGY AND SPIRIT

Energy is powerful, yes, but it is manageable. In nature, energy is constantly metamorphosing. It is the very nature of energy to be in motion, ever changing, always active, performing, transforming. The basis of technology is turning one form of energy into another—motion into electricity, for example, fossils into heat, heat into motion.

Even our thoughts, as subtle as they are, are capable of transforming energy. Thoughts, as we know, can mobilize energy, align it, move it, and magnify it.

An organization's energy—its vim, vigor, power, and so forth—is managed by changing the intensity and direction of energy. We inject energy, release it, expand it, and funnel it. In fact, that's an excellent definition of good management/leadership: arousing and channeling a human system's energy, infusing *oomph.*

On the other hand, Spirit, as it's being used here (big-*S* Spirit), does *not* change! Spirit is immutable; Spirit is that which always remains the same. Always.

At that, the mind, which is worldly connected, spins and leaps. How can that be? Science tells us that everything changes! The hardest of rocks wear away, turning ultimately to dust. Even diamonds change, given enough time. All energy decomposes into another form of energy—and everything is energy, isn't it? Therefore, all is in movement, in constant vibration. Everything in the world is constantly changing!

Spirit, however, is beyond all that! That's the point. It is beyond the natural world, so it's beyond time and the consequences of time. It's beyond science as we know it. Spirit is beyond nature, so it is beyond the causes and effects of the natural universe. It doesn't have a nature.

But energy does. Energy is of the world and in the world. Everything in the world is energy. Spirit, however, isn't in the world. Spirit is the *Source* of it all. Spirit is cause. It's the "whence," remember. It's always there—unmoving, unmovable.

Let's apply this thinking to the illness experience. Spirit really is beyond the body, unchanged and unchanging. Even as my physical self was being bombarded and battered, there was still an inner something watching, observing. That inner being (call it Spirit) remained unhurt and unshaken throughout the onslaught. The body was sick, but the Spirit wasn't even touched!

Back to the question of managing Spirit: if Spirit is unchanging, then how do we manage it? The answer: we don't. We manage ourselves or our organizations in relation to Spirit. We try to become ready for it. We work to develop a capacity for it, an openness to it. It's a mega-allowing. We nurture a reverence for Spirit and cultivate the humility to receive it. In effect, Spirit reenters us, even though it had never really left.

What I just described may imply a "tapping into" Spirit, but it's really more like turning to face it, or uncovering it. We move to realize Spirit, and embrace it. We follow the directions from within to move closer to Spirit and avail ourselves of the resultant energy. Like that Native American ideal in chapter 2, we live in constant spiritual awareness and reap the energy that comes from being more whole. That's how we "manage" it.

Spirit, we saw, is the rock, not the wavy lines. When we move to Spirit, it's as though we journey high, high into another realm—a quiet, mysterious region. We're in the domain of Universal Source, the Cosmic Self department. This is the place of *That* which breathes life into matter. This is home of basic Life itself, not the signs of it, for the signs are energy and we're beyond energy here.

As I arrive at this high place, there's a hushed awe in me, a calm wonder. Peace. I feel deep respect and reverence and gratitude . . . and yet, almost impish. The memories of alien invaders storming the gates during my illness are now dim memories. There's a happiness in me and, because of that, there's a quiet laugh close to my surface. I feel fortunate and blessed, vigorously alive here in this rare space, beyond vitality, at Spirit.

PART II

REVERING

LOVE AND REVERENCE IN WORK AND LIFE

T his part addresses a cornerstone spiritual value: deep caring for others—a respect so intense it becomes reverence. We carefully walk up to what love, the "L-word" in business, actually means, and whether or not it is relevant in the workplace.

CHAPTER 4

THE REVERENCE CONTINUUM
IN ORGANIZATIONS

> *Energy comes from the heart
> expanding. Small, closed heart,
> no energy.*
>
> —Sathya Sai Baba

Reverence is the one ingredient in the new management stew that everyone loves but can't seem to pin down. This is the loving secret sauce. This is what gives the stew its heart, its goodness.

Nevertheless, people feel funny about this ingredient. They're shy about it. Too often it's left out. Yet it's not very mysterious and certainly is not rare. This is the most common and mightiest of the powerful new/ancient forces available to today's managers. Reverence is the power that's pulling the new management paradigm. It's the very reason the new stew is cooking.

THE REVERENCE REACH

I'm in the boardroom of a new client company, talking to the management group about "personality patterns" in organizations. It's an interesting company, founded by a good-hearted Hollywood movie star to create jobs for people from the ghettos and barrios of Los Angeles. But the professional managers running the company are in a hard-fought industry and the company is in trouble. I'm reaching to make a point.

41

I walk to the chalkboard and draw a horizontal line, planning to use it for showing a range of behavior in organizations. I say, "There's a reverence continuum in organizations." I'm a little surprised when the word *reverence* comes out and notice a few brows wrinkling and some quizzical looks. How did I get into this?

A few months previously a woman from India had come to stay with us and our five teenagers. She was a bright shining lady, a woman who had gained some extra capacities to "see" in ways that many of us don't. There was something special in her ways: a veneration of seemingly worldly things that brought learning to others.

She told us how her father taught her and her siblings to treat *all* things—not only people—with deference and respect; he even included objects that form part of one's household. Little acts, like opening a door, for example: "Don't just yank it and barge through," he taught. "Turn the knob slowly, swing the door along its arch carefully, have reverence for it." Reverence for a door?! I noticed our offspring exchange glances behind their politeness.

"Even eating an apple," she said on another occasion. "We were taught not to gobble it, but to hold it lovingly in both hands and give thanks for the gift of sweetness and nourishment it so freely offers." At that, son Alec, who usually inhaled apples, wrinkled his brow and glanced at the waxy macintosh in his hand.

Our airy kitchen enchanted her and her cooking soon cast a spell over us. It didn't take long for her to sweep the meat and eggs from the fridge, but she did it so sensitively and with such a logic that we welcomed it. After preparing delicious vegetable stews (curries), she would quietly chant the prayer and set aside her first morsel as an offering of gratitude. Her subtle examples began to seep into us all.

Christmas season came and enveloped the family. We were all, as was our custom each year, dancing to the stressful strains of the holiday hustle-bustle, scurrying our separate ways, meeting only on rare occasions. One day I walk in, breathless as usual. Louise is also there, having just arrived with a new Christmas wreath. "Nice," I say. "We've got five minutes. Let's hang it." I grab hammer and nails. She grabs the wreath. We zip out to the front door.

Our Indian lady is there with us, totally enthralled with the wreath. "Oh, it's so beautiful, so green," she gushes, "such a wonderful symbol. Oh, see how the leaves and berries exist together . . . oh, how gorgeous." "Yeah," I say, motioning for Louise to hold it in place on the door. Bang, bang. "There, done," I smirk. I pivot to return to the house and, Oops!, almost trip over the Indian lady. She's doing a *namaskar* (kneeling on the patio, forehead to the cement, hands joined out in front of her), intoning a special blessing toward the wreath!

What do you do when a friend is kneeling at your feet directing prayers at your holly? Do you ignore her and tiptoe away, step over her and risk stumbling? Do you kneel with her? Having never encountered the issue before, we just stand a little self-consciously, waiting for her to finish. And we wait, and wait—one minute, two minutes, three. While positioned there, waiting, I come down a little from the frenetic pace and the world becomes a little quieter. Indeed, now that I notice it, she's right about the wreath: it really is a beautiful thing, and what it represents is even more so.

What's more, as we stand there, her blessing seems to work! The wreath becomes imbued with something more significant than simply being a decoration. For four full minutes (a long time nowadays) I stand there; the wreath is on the door at my shoulder. As I do, I begin to feel something more from it—a specialness, a power that I was unaware of before.

And that power lasts throughout the holidays. Gradually the family pace becomes less hurried. As the calm grows, so does our appreciation of the season. And each time I pass the wreath, I feel that "something" reach out and touch my shoulder.

It was with these vibrations still in me that I resumed working in January and found myself having drawn a "reverence" line on the chalkboard in front of the group of furrow-browed managers. As I said, I'm a bit surprised that the word *reverence* came out, but I've seen those kinds of brows before and trust what's happening.

I proceed with my talk, explaining that an organization's basic personality can be plotted somewhere along this line, this continuum, depending on the general pattern of human relationships within it.

Then I draw two short vertical strokes about a third of the way along the line (as illustrated below). "Call this the dividing plane between basically uncivilized and basically civilized organizations," I say. "To the left are those without real human relationships. They're generally mean-spirited, indifferent, and apathetic. Unfortunately, there are many of them, but disregard them for now and consider only organizations that are basically civilized."

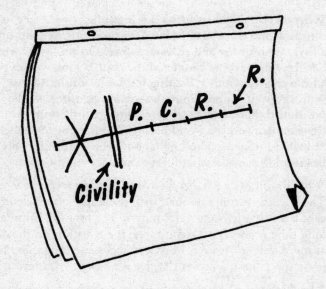

I then divide the line to the right of this plane into four segments. "Let's look at some gradations of civility." I point to the first segment. "The most elementary civilized organizational personality is the Polite Organization, wherein people are at least minimally considerate and attentive to one another." I label this segment *P*. "These are organizations with manners; there's a whiff of common courtesy in the air there."

I think, and reach for an example: "The English as a nation are generally good at this. Even if they don't like you, they'll at least act politely toward you most of the time. It may be forced and thinly veiled, but they seldom let themselves dip below a minimum level of civility.

"But Polite Organizations better be careful," I caution. "If they persist in acting that way and thus become compulsively polite, they will become distanced, separated from real feelings of any sort, and this will deaden them to improvement.

"On the other hand, if Polite Organizations really want to improve, again they had better be careful," I say half jokingly, "because if they persist in their politeness, it will grow and will slip over the line into real caring. The Caring Organization is the Polite Organization that's even more so." I scratch a *C* in the next segment.

"In the Caring Organization members are more concerned and more attentive. They're generally more interested in people and their work, and are more thoughtful. In this organization you see them watching out for one another, for the organization—and for customers. There's a heightened consciousness in this type of company that's really noticeable. People *care* more; that's good for them and their clients, and everybody likes it."

I give as an example a particular high-production pharmacy unit in a huge medical center. The unit operates as a human prescription-filling machine. You walk in and all heads are down, paying attention to business, churning out thousands upon thousands of medications each day. There's a whole squad of pharmacists behind a glass partition busily filling prescriptions, and there's a score of clerks working the front end of the human "machine," pecking at computer terminals and handling the throngs of patients coming to the long counter. One day, a while back, an elderly man shuffled slowly up to the counter and asked in a weak, shaky voice for diabetes medicine. Every head in the unit looked up to make sure the patient wasn't "in trouble."

With this example the wrinkled brows of the management group have smoothed out some; their faces aren't quite as quizzical; it's beginning to make sense. I continue, a bit lighter, "But Caring Organizations better watch out because those behaviors, too, become a habit. If they're not careful, care grows into respect." I label the third segment *R*.

"Respect. Imagine an organization climate soaked in respect. Respect is one of those qualities you all know when you feel it, and especially when you don't; yet it's not something that's thought about or talked about much," I continue.

"What are the important human interactions and feelings that make up a respectful environment?" I then ask. The group helps build the list: Consideration toward one another. Holding others in esteem. Admiration. Genuine politeness. Kindness. Valuing others. People "liking" each other. It's a good list. "That's the kind of organization I hear people all over calling for," I say.

Now they know where I'm heading, they shift a little in their seats. I go ahead anyway, "Respect can become a habit, too; if and when it eventually deepens, it becomes reverence." An *R* goes in the last segment. Here's how the completed chart looked.

The Reverence Continuum in Organizations

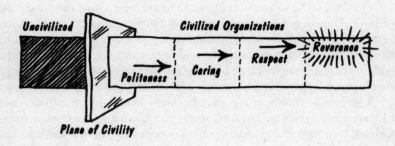

The wrinkles and quizzical looks have returned, furrows etched deeper. I might have backed off here and tried to smooth things, but something prompts me to persevere. "I know reverence sounds far out"— I pause a moment—"but think back to the best boss you've ever worked for or the best team you've ever worked on or the best subordinates you've ever worked with." I encourage them to pause, turn inward, and take a full minute to do their recollecting.

I time it—sixty quiet, precious seconds—then continue, "Tell me, was there reverence in that situation?" Certainly! Every forehead in the room immediately nods agreement. It's a revelation to themselves (and even to me); reverence *is* more common in the workplace than we think.

WHAT IS REVERENCE?

What does *reverence* actually mean? Pious muttering in a darkened place on weekends? No. Reverence consists of dedication, eagerness, and enthusiasm. There's deep admiration and respect in it. There's devotedness, if not outright devotion, in it. There's deep conviction and earnestness in it, too. Foreign? Not really. These are the qualities of great organizations! Think about it. Reverence is an intensified state of commitment—and commitment is the grail that managers are eternally seeking.

Hold a candle nearer to reverence: you see fondness, you detect deep appreciation and gratitude. Step even closer: veneration, which is high caring, appears. Taking it to the level of veneration is what brings the intensity required to build great human organizations.

Ask a person, How's your organization? Do they tell you about last week's widget yield or this year's return on investment? Neither. They answer how they feel about the humanness of the organization, and their answers fit on a continuum like the one I've just been describing. They may not think of or talk about affection, caring, respect, devotedness, and so forth, but they sure feel those things.

These aren't just softheaded emotions. These are, as we have said, what great organizations are made of. And the ideas embedded in reverence aren't only emotions—they're more than feelings—they're energies. Combined, these ideas that make up reverence are a force, a power.

This is the mighty stuff that magnifies meaning, and it's just waiting to be called. Superb managers know this and learn to use it for the betterment of the organization. We should watch the Japanese (and a growing number of fine organizations elsewhere) to pick up their vaunted management "secret." To put it simply: develop a reverence—no less than that—for: (a) the mission, (b) the products, (c) the customers, and (d) the employees. Such great companies carry commitment and dedication to the lofty elevation of devotion. The overarching point is reverence.

On that account, we can now spot reverence as a key component of excellent management nowadays. Surprising? A little perhaps, but remember: this is the new stew we're stirring.

CHAPTER 5

RESPECT, CARING, AND BIG LOVING

Love all, serve all.
— Pocket logo, Hard Rock
Cafe sweatshirt

I meet Isaac in India of all places. He and two friends—an American living in France and a fellow from Tennessee—are trying to charter a plane from Bangalore to Allahabad. Chartering a plane in India is undreamed of. People don't have the money for it, or if they do, they don't care to get there that fast.

But Isaac has the money for it. Despite longish hair and smiling blue eyes that communicate a sort of graduate hippie, he's a seasoned executive accustomed to international travel. And he doesn't have to worry about paying for the charter. He has just completed the sale of his nineteen-year-old business for about $107 million. That might not be very big money to Unilever or General Motors, but to a forty-year-old businessman from the southern United States, it's ample proof that following your heart pays off.

Isaac was raised in a rich family in the South in the 1960s. His hometown was 90 percent black. Like other southern cities at that time, it was rigidly, ironhandedly segregated. Such policies deeply offended this sensitive teenager who was already an outspoken advocate for human fairness. In those days in the States that meant that he was close to the civil rights movement.

"Then," he says in his quiet, sincere way, "the civil rights law passed and they took down the segregation signs. Made a big impression on me. Talk about symbolism! Those signs were blatant emblems of classism [he uses classism and racism interchangeably]. They were constant reminders to the majority of people—black people—in that city that they weren't as good as others. Then—*swoosh*—the signs are gone! All of a sudden people—all of us, not just blacks—are more human." He shakes his head in wonder even now, after all these years.

When Isaac's parents divorced, he chose to go to England with his father. By then he felt close to the new consciousness sweeping the world. Rather than the university, he went to work in one of his dad's factories in northern England.

"And was that an education! It didn't just make an impression on me, it was so deep it dented me!" he says. Once, he led a wildcat strike against management. The key issue was noise, and this strike was more than just shouting slogans. "Hey," his voice rises as he recalls the clamor, "those machines in my father's factory were so loud that people were going deaf, and management wouldn't even listen to them!" [The poetry of it: "Goin' deaf and the boss won't hear."]

After that, Isaac made some money buying old Rolls Royces for resale in the States. But his social conscience was still in the driver's seat. On Bond Street one day he watched a bobby routinely roust a lad who, from his cap and demeanor, didn't belong out of the East End. Isaac still burns, "That was the epitome of the Victorian class system. The kid couldn't even go to the other side of town without being shooed back to his proper place!"

He sets his jaw and continues, with the usual quiet sincerity in his voice. "In England in those days the social classes were still completely separated. There was literally no place in London where a baker and a banker could meet to talk. They each had their own eating establishments, their own clubs or pubs; they simply never came together." Apparently that "dented" him too. "I wanted to break that system," he says, his zealousness showing through the quiet. *Break it!*—that's revolutionary language.

So, this young idealist, not yet twenty, not really accomplished at anything other than deeply caring for other human beings, decides to open a restaurant with a friend—an absolutely classless restaurant. He flies back to the States, uses the family name to wangle a $60,000 loan from hometown bankers, returns to London, and rents space in the middle of ultrafancy Mayfair.

At that time, London was the heart of the new consciousness movement, a sort of headquarters of transformational thinking. The movement was youth-based and youth-oriented. The young people talked a lot about "love." Their heroes were musicians. "Music was politics, not just popular songs," says Isaac.

He capitalizes on all those energies. He opens the first blatantly American restaurant in England—in Europe, in the world—that is associated with "the movement": the Hard Rock Cafe. The basic concept is a friendly Tennessee truck stop, right in the middle of London. It's his blow for equality on the planet.

The dream (the ideas as well as the ideals), the timing, the city, and the place itself couldn't have been more appropriate. From opening day it's a smashing success. Standing in line waiting for tables are the bankers and the bakers, the taxi drivers and the executives, the blue collars and the white. These are the souls who people the system he's out to break, and they're readily participating in the breaking.

Also coming to the restaurant from the start are the movement's heroes, now allies: Jimi Hendrix, Cream, the Beatles, the Stones, and all the others. People love the restaurant. It's an instantly famous happening.

Isaac had pledged that if he ever got the opportunity to run a business, he wouldn't do it like any he had ever seen. "I was the third- or fourth-youngest person in the place and knew nothing about the restaurant business, so I had to follow my heart," he says. "There simply weren't any guidelines for creating the kind of place I had in my mind and heart."

He personally hires every one of the employees. "My rainbow collection," he calls them. "We had twenty-five native languages on the staff." He holds daily, and then weekly, "family meetings" with the entire staff. "Teach me this business," he tells them, "and I'll provide the resources and the rudder."

The staff meetings are wild and full of energy. "We train and train some more," he says. "Every week, we talk about kindness, about quality through politeness, and about our themes: classlessness and 'aggressive American friendliness.' We have to work to offset the usual English reserve. We want the place to exude love."

Isaac institutes the first profit-sharing plan in a restaurant company in England. Profits are doled out to every employee based on a scoring system that includes friendliness, helpfulness, and fitting into the "family," as well as more conventional work-performance items. Everybody is treated equally. Normally, women in the sixties were paid exactly half of men's wages; at the Hard Rock they're paid exactly the same.

At about that time Isaac hears of a powerful holy man in India: Sai Baba. Wanting some reassurance that this idealistic path he has chosen is the right one—a path that he sees as a spiritual adventure as well as a worldly one—Isaac wonders whether Baba might give him some guidance.

The pull to go to India is strong. Despite being terribly busy, he arranges things and hops a plane to India. When he gets there, Baba smiles at him and that's all. "Huh! Nine thousand miles for one of those smiles?" Isaac, in a hurry as usual, has to sit and cool his heels for two weeks. He asks, he pleads for a private talk with Baba, but he doesn't even get another smile! He picks himself up, dusts off his hands, and hops on the London plane. "Oh well," he philosophizes, "it was a good couple of weeks. I know I got something of value even if I'm not sure exactly what it was."

"You won't find a more *dharmic* manager than me," he laughs. "I knew everybody at the restaurant by name and everybody knew me. And they all had my phone number and knew they could contact me directly at any time. I spent 70 percent of my time on the phone. The employees and I had a special relationship. Later I even put Fax machines in each of the employee lounges, direct to my office. Every employee in every Hard Rock Cafe in the world knew he or she could contact me personally any time.

"I empowered certain people as 'management' or 'supervisors,' and then helped them not abuse that power. I held them responsible for business matters—and accountable as human beings, too. Whether through ego or ignorance or simply habit, if their actions went counter to what we were aiming for in our work environment, it became an opportunity for me to provide some 'special help' to them! They absolutely knew where I was coming from.

"I gave the personnel manager power to overrule the general manager, for example, in matters of heart and common courtesy—pay shortages or advances before a holiday, things like that. These people are restaurant workers, they don't make much money; the least we can do is be sensitive and stretch a little for them. Respect was the key. We respected people and expected respect in return.

"And the same goes for customers," he continues. Then he explains that because of his own aversion to waiting in lines, he felt a special concern for the people in the long lines always outside the front door. "I hated seeing people in a queue in bad weather," he laments. "But what can you do? We talked about it a lot in our meetings and finally hit on an elegant idea.

"We decided to extend the boundary of our restaurant to the end of the waiting line, wherever that was, and sometimes it was way around the park. We didn't consult lawyers or any

of that stuff, we just proclaimed it. We appointed a Queue
Maitre d'. He was constantly out there making people more
comfortable. He would bring out umbrellas in rainy weather
(and we never lost one); when it was hot, iced tea, and when
it was icy, cocoa or soup. That sort of captures how it was,"
he says. "Everybody loved the place!"

Isaac's eyes light up when he talks about the company.
"Being one of the Hard Rock Cafe family was therapy for
people. Even if they came from a violent home life, here they
were loved, and they loved back in return.

"People always do. I could hire those no one else would take,
and in six or seven months they'd be new people. I called it
my 'High School' and I told 'em I wanted everyone to
graduate. I realized early on that we were creating habits,
that's all, just habits. That's what success or failure in life
comes from: habits. So I determined to create good ones. We
graduated some great souls.

"Everybody loved the place," he repeats, beaming, "everybody felt bigger working there. We were famous. Just walk
into the place and this great energy hit you immediately.
Employees were proud of the place, from the dishwasher on
up." He uses the words *spirit, love, dharma,* and *energy* as
though they are interchangeable.

After he got back from his India trip, it struck him: "If we're
so famous, if people love the Hard Rock so much, why not
take that and reflect it back at them with a message?" So he
started printing epigrams on paychecks, T-shirts, sweatshirts,
and such. They were little aphorisms he had gotten in India:
"Start the day with love" "Do good, be good, see good" and
so forth. "I sold millions of sweatshirts to lots of different
kinds of people—some of them pretty rough," he says with
an impish gleam, "and on every one of them was that sign:
Love all, serve all. That must've done some good!"

Here we have Isaac talking dharma, love, spirit, and energy—all huge
ideas, all dumped into the same mixing bowl. Also in the bowl, of course,
are the qualities of integrity, courage, inner truth, affection, politeness,
caring, respect, intensity, and power, to name but a few. This matter of

reverence is obviously a huge, important subject, and also a disorderly one.

Let's stick our faces closer to the reverence bowl and examine this mixture. Maybe it sorts into something more, well, businesslike. We can get back to Isaac after a while.

Chapter 6

Shyness about the "L-word" in Business: *Love*

If respect and reverence can be such an effective way of operating a business, why are businesspeople so reluctant to acknowledge the legitimacy of love in their organizations? Other professionals—social scientists, hard scientists, doctors, teachers, and so forth—have this same reluctance. Why do people shy away and act as though love, this wondrous, crucial idea, doesn't exist? Hmmm. Intriguing. I encounter this reluctance all over and have even experienced it myself. What is behind it?

I scratch my head and sit quietly. For some unknown reason my thoughts drift to my inner experience of Japan. When I go there, I feel good. I greatly admire the people and culture, and I'm especially taken with their politeness and respectfulness.

But I'm also aware that I feel a little manipulated when I'm there. It's soft and subtle. It's as though I can't quite be myself. They're so polite that I have to be also even if I don't feel that way. It's not that I'm impolite; I just like having the freedom to be. In Japan, because of the incessant courteousness, I don't feel that freedom. Do they feel the same in reverse when they come to the West?

Louise, who is unshamefacedly warm and loving, says she occasionally feels people pull away from her because of this trait. They don't know how to take her forwardness. Maybe to them it's gushy and they feel forced into acting that way; maybe they're shy.

Here's a story that illustrates some of the complexities embedded in this shyness about the "L-word."

A group of executives in the Midwest is discussing the general reluctance to talk about feelings of caring toward others in their companies. They, too, are hesitant to get into it; there's a long, uneasy silence. One of the female executives finally smiles, swallows, and begins speaking . . .

"This is the most important thing we can talk about, that's why I've been quiet. This subject really perplexes me. I'm a loving person, but I just can't see how you can be loving on the job. And I feel bad when I'm not."

Her opening gives permission to the others. One man speaks up and the others recover their tongues.

"Yeah, but when love and affection and all those softhearted things are talked about, either I agree or I'm labeled unfeeling. Love is laid on you as new dogma, as a stack of new rules. You get signals to disregard your old self and become a new, softer self. Unless you're a 'lover,' you're a lout. Love can be very manipulative!"

"Frankly, what does love have to do with profit objectives, forecasts, productivity, and such? Sure, love and reverence are important, but do they really belong in organizations?"

This line of discussion continues for some time. The general tone of the comments reflects a respect for the topic and an awareness that there's a mighty idea working here and it's only dimly understood. Eventually they point to some demanding questions:

How do you act lovingly without feeling foolish or weird?

How can you be caring without being seen as weak, without being taken advantage of?

What about those times when you have to act unlovingly, when you have to take control, or take command? And

what about those times when you have to push hard—
when you simply must win, when you have to fly in the
face of opposition? What if it's your job to win?

How can you act lovingly when your job calls for you to
be a tiger, when your role is that of a "business gladiator"?
What do you do if you're (check one): a lawyer, an
auditor, a sales manager, a contract administrator, a
buyer, a mediator, a troubleshooter, a labor negotiator,
a union president, an army general?

What about when you must make decisions that cause
pain and disruption, that result in people losing their
jobs or being forced to relocate? What about decisions
that you know others won't like and will probably fight?
Aren't pain and fighting contrary to loving?

How about the times you have to enforce a regulation,
correct bad habits, or otherwise discipline people? And
what about those times when you've played all your
cards and simply have to look someone in the eye and
deliver an ultimatum, or even fire them. Is that loving?

And what about the times you have to play the role of
"the great leader," when you simply have to assert the
power of your office, be the boss—when the buck stops
at your desk and you are the final authority? Is that
loving?

I listen to their words and try to react not to the intellectual
content but to the feelings in them. Between the lines I hear
these people caught in the grip of a so-called love that's really
untrue—or at best is a tiny fraction of truth. They are
"lovingly" directed to care and express affection, and this
notice is fed to them sugarcoated so they can't contest it.
What do they do? Sham agree and flee into silence.

And so people (us) run from this stupendous force, this handle-on-the-
world force: love. We escape from being forced into it, shying from what
we feel as being poisoned or smothered. We're fearful our self will be cut

away, and this danger is real to us, no matter that we may have narrow perceptions of love. We feel forced to bury our true self under a mask of pleasantries. Thus the real truth of love is stifled.

"They implore us to love," we say, "and we can't." And there's no way out of this quandary because it is in *not* loving where real smothering occurs. Yet, the only love many of us see is a coerced love, which is a love born of fear and rooted in attachment, an earthbound, unfree love.

Love, if directed by others, can't be love. It's another's will imposed in the name of something great, rather than something from within. Such "love" is a form of violence in soft garb, a cloaked denial of the other. It is often the only way people know. This compelled love is about as sincere and loving as many people ever experience.

So where's the exit? How can we escape? Can this facade-love lift faces of stone? For a while, perhaps, but those forced smiles steal people's energy until there's none left. Is it possible to turn away completely, spinning into hate, one of love's opposites? No, not if you want to live a happy life. Can you crawl into another opposite—apathy? Perhaps. It may hurt less, but it brings the habit of emptiness and earns a deathlike existence.

So we stumble along trying to vanish into "toughness," unaware that real love resides there also. And too often we fall into the real opposite of love: fear. We lumber through life at a pace fast enough not to get caught by heavy love, and the real thing is effortlessly pacing beside us all the way. Though elbow to elbow with it, brushing against it, we seldom recognize it.

CHAPTER 7

THE SIX LANDSCAPES OF LOVE

Mother Teresa won a Nobel Prize for her loving. The academy called it a Peace Prize, but we all know it was awarded for her great ability to love.

In her talks she refers to "the science of love." It's a nice metaphor for today, conveying the important idea that love should receive serious attention. I'm sure she doesn't mean "science" literally, though. Trying to make love precise, replicable, and measurable would shrink it down and shrivel it up in short order. But her point is clear: we must give love the same close attention we give other things these days; we must move nearer to love and become better at it.

But that's easier said than done. Trying to take in the entire scenery of love is a dizzying experience. The vastness of these ideas and ideals is breathtaking. How might we breathe in this boundless, colossal subject? By parceling it into smaller breaths.

THE SIX LANDSCAPES OF LOVE

First, we sort love into six parcels, as shown in the illustration on the next page: love as desire, as feelings, as action, as giving, as energy, and love as spirit. Then, we array the parcels next to one another, stair-stepped according to a rough idea of intensity and scope.

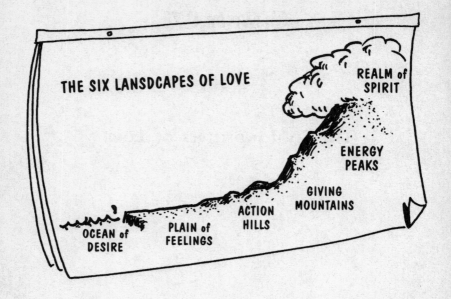

THE SIX LANSDCAPES OF LOVE

REALM of SPIRIT

ENERGY PEAKS

GIVING MOUNTAINS

ACTION HILLS

PLAIN of FEELINGS

OCEAN of DESIRE

Love as Desire *(Wanting Love)*

We're in the first parcel. What looked like drab sameness from high above is really a choppy, gray-green sea. The first "landscape" turns out to be a seascape: the Ocean of Desire. It's vast—we'll need to spend a while here.

This is the world of: Oh, I'd *love* to have that. Oh, I *loved* that movie. Oh, I *love* profits. Oh, I *love* you; come to me, baby. Here the word *love* is bandied around loosely. The problem is that all of what is called love isn't really love, it's something else. Most often it's desire and attachment, or covetousness, or "ownership," or whatever.

It's the same word, *love,* but the world it is used in is often the exact opposite of love. Grasping, craving, possessiveness, and envy live here. Oh, there may be times of happiness in this world; but if we analyze our experience of love here, we realize that they're only the spaces between unhappiness. There may be enjoyment here, but curiously, it's not joy. There might even be satisfaction here; it's short-lived, however, and leads not to contentment but to dissatisfaction.

The Ocean of Desire is teeming with voracious creatures named Wanting and Acquiring, Owning and Possessing. Oddly, even though it's a world based on attachment, beings here are isolated from one another. "That's yours and this is mine" is the law here. But real love contains no ties that bind. There's none of this kind of desire in genuine love. The "love" here is a simulated pearl.

Life in this fake place centers around indulgence of self; small-*s*, worldly, material self. People forget their higher selves and chase things and activities that yield worldly pleasure. Gratification, gold, and other glitzy goodies are the grails here. Hankerings become necessities. When one desire is satisfied, another rises to take its place.

This world is offshore from real love. Remember the frightful island Pinocchio was taken to when he ran away to become a real boy? I can see it now. At first, it looked like a fun park: everybody smoking, drinking, and gambling—really enjoying themselves. Remember? But the people lured there gradually turn into donkeys with their hands and feet becoming hooves. Then, they are whipped and harnessed to freight wagons, where we see them ultimately sweating and straining under crushing loads.

But not our "Pinoke." When he begins to sprout donkey ears and tail, he knows this place isn't for him. He barely manages to escape into the sea before becoming a complete ass. "Hooray!" we cheer. But nobody laments those other poor lads, now beasts of burden, doomed to sweating and straining for life!

There's a greed-grief link in this love as desire.

I recall sitting with lawyer friend, Grant. We're at "his" table in a fancy restaurant in Los Angeles. He tugs at his gold cuff links, obviously uncomfortable. His face is sad behind his composed mask. In a voice to match his face he asks, "Where's it all end?" He stares into the space over my shoulder and shakes his head in dismay.

Long silences ensue except for the sound of his swirling drink, ice cubes racing frantically around the glass. "We moved into a 7,000-square-foot house, leaving the old house which was 'only' 5,000 square feet. My first wife calls up and tells me she's going back to court to fight for an increase in her alimony. My [current] wife wants another car . . . I'm breaking my hump, straining to keep all these hoops [he might have said wagons] rolling—and I know it's all unreal."

Constantly hungering for possessions becomes a habit. Accumulation and ownership become a way of life. After a while, people simply don't think of alternatives. These habits are insidious addictions—people are hooked on things and conditions that they have been conditioned to want. It's compulsive behavior; they simply can't stop doing it! "But I *love* the new house," says the current wife. Does she really mean that, or is this but a rampaging habit?

Greed also swims in this sea—Jawslike, an open maw, gliding through this watery environment; a voracious, streamlined consuming machine, swallowing all in its path. And where greed swims, so do covetousness, craving, selfishness, jealousy, and manipulation.

Fear swims here, too. The whole environment smells of fear, not love. People fearing loss—of possessions, of position, of prestige, of self-respect, even of self—and people fearing the next bout with sorrow, which inevitably swims with all these "self-fish." And yet, they continue the pattern of workaholism and buyaholism, frantically straining toward happiness.

Also floating throughout this sea is a dark, powerful force, fear's blood kin: anger. The term *blinding anger* is apt. Anger spurts a cloud of darkness, rendering people visionless, unable to see the reality of their lives. Fear and anger, always together; you never have one without the other. As one fattens, so does the other—to the point where you can't tell one from the other. The environment reeks of this fear-anger, not love.

On and on it goes, with people's very lives being devoured. Endless greed resulting in endless grief; craving turning into raving; needing into weeping. It all brings ceaseless sorrow and emptiness. Life becomes endless bouts of greed and grief, strong enough to bring people to their knees, tears to their eyes, stunned, shaking their heads, asking, Where's it going to end?

The Buddha knows where it ends. You know him—an oriental-looking statue, blissfully meditating. It may come as a surprise but he wasn't interested in religion; he was a great practical psychologist. His main regard was human happiness. His message was (is) very simple: you *can* eradicate sorrow! Yep. Say good-bye to anguish, pain, and suffering.

His great contribution is the idea that all sorrow that afflicts mankind, yes, *all* sorrow on this planet, stems from one thing: desire. It makes a neat equation: $d = s$, desire equals sorrow. That's the greed-grief link. Remove one, the other vanishes. Simple idea, but it's not easy. Habits are powerful here in nonlove country.

Love as Feelings (Emotional Love)

We leave this vast, murky area to continue on our heart mission, rising above the rocky shores to clear the cliffs, soaring over a grassy plain. There's great beauty here—richness, abundance, a big sky, far horizons. Here we see love as a cluster of emotions, thoughts, and attitudes. The key idea is love as the *feeling* of love. Love in this place consists of fairly straightforward, open, bright, upbeat feelings. This is the love we're reminded of when the word is used.

This love is most recognizable as the feeling of love between people, but often it extends beyond that. Some of the ingredients in the feeling are deep fondness, fascination, and attraction. It's a supermagnified liking of somebody—liking them so much your breath and heart are affected. It's that quickening, that catch in your throat when the other comes into the room.

Usually people think of love in twos, as when two people are "in" it and feel it toward one another. This kind of love is woven into our culture. We've heard thousands of love songs thousands of times each. The words constantly go around in our heads, programming, shaping. We've seen countless love stories played before us throughout our lives. This is the many-splendored thing. And most important, we're actors in our own love stories, forever playing out our own dramas of love. That's a key thread in the fabric of our lives: the continuing love story that is us!

Like separate facets on a giant gemstone, each of the feelings of love shines its magnificence upon the world. Compassion lives here, as does sympathy. Also here are the feelings of dedication, forgiving, brotherhood, and togetherness. The feeling of sincerity resides here. So do believing in and respect. The feeling of commitment and the feeling of loyalty are here, too, as are feelings of deep affection and compelling attraction.

When we feel dignity, we're feeling an aspect of this landscape of love. When we feel innocence or guilelessness or simplicity, we are experiencing this love. This is wondrous quintessential stuff, this love as feelings.

Notice that there's not much room in this landscape for feelings of desire or *amour* or fondling. They're strong feelings, and they're often called by the name of love, but they're really not. "I love profits" is a far cry from "I love you," but they're often used in a way that means about the same: yearning and possession. When used this way, it's not really love. Pure love is not possessive. Desire-based love may be great for the short run, but it isn't a high, lasting love. The desires may even be quite gentle and relatively harmless, but nonetheless they're desires, and real love isn't desire, remember.

This often happens with such bandied words. The word *love* has become so all-inclusive in its meanings that we use it for more mundane items: "I love that painting." Well, maybe you do, but that sounds more like art appreciation or an expression of enjoyment.

Friend Bill, an Englishman, finds it hard to accept the idea that love might be quite simple; he prefers to make a more distant and unattainable thing of it. All these years he's thought of himself as a nonloving chap—even though feelings of loneliness and emptiness accompany that thought. "My heart is closed," he would sigh.

But when love is defined to Bill as just rather everyday feelings, when the list of these understandable, quite ordinary feelings is actually read to him—compassion, liking, kindness, and so forth—there's an uncomfortable rapping on his closed-door heart. The possibility that he has, all these years, been more loving than he thought—that his feelings of deep caring and respect for others may be this thing called love—seems to embarrass him. "Oh, that's love?" he mumbles, looking away.

Love as Action (Doing Love)

Still appreciating the uncomplicated notion of love as feelings, we move on, determined to carry out our mission. Soon the level country begins to roll—easily at first, and then more, until we're in a region of foothills spotted with greenery and small groves of trees. Here we have scenic beauty, variety, and light.

These are the Action Hills. This is the landscape where love is defined as actually doing love. In this country, love is the daily acts of love that living beings perform. There's quite a difference between these hills and the plains. Actions usually involve other people and are quite evident, whereas feelings are individual, mostly internal, and can be invisible.

This is the landscape of action, where people perform kindness, giving, helping, sharing, being patient, and tolerant. Action-oriented people embrace this definition—there's substance in it. "In all the great literatures," observes consultant-psychologist Steven Covey (1990), "love is a verb." The feeling of love derives from the acts of love. To love activists, this is "where the rubber meets the road." Love, to them, is *doing*, not just feeling.

What before were considered nice sentiments within individuals—feelings of brotherhood, sisterhood, and togetherness, for example—now appear as *acts* of friendliness, helping, and team play. Forgiveness is actually rendered, it is conveyed, and the recipient experiences it. People here don't just feel friendliness, they *are* it—reaching out, serving, displaying thoughtfulness. Similarly, feelings of unity and amity in organizations appear here as acts of cooperation, helping, caring, sharing, and understanding. This is where the sentiments emerge as actual behavior.

The appeal of an acting-out brand of love is understandable. In many ways the love activists are right: this really is where the rubber meets the road.

Love as Giving (Selfless Love)

We continue our mission, moving beyond the goodness of worldly actions and feelings, closer to the heart of love. The rolling hills become steeper. Then, quite suddenly, they thrust sharply upward, like huge hands abruptly stretched toward the heavens, craggy fingers bathed in bright light, reaching for and touching the sky, as though in this landscape love is connecting beyond the world. We're in the towering Selfless Mountains.

Closer to the peaks, something is different. There's a naturalness, a simplicity. We've left some baggage behind. Ah, breathe in the purity of this place, the heady aroma of freedom. There's less fear now. Here love has no strings attached. It's just given freely. This is one-way love country: love is just given with no expectations of return in it. Imagine! Just given—like the apple tree gives apples because it's its nature to give. This is the land of pure love. Love here is unsullied, unalloyed with desires. Nothing is required in return, it's absolutely free, and it's almost unheard of nowadays.

People are conditioned from tender years to "use" love. Love therefore becomes a lever or an investment. People learn early that love is a game of give and get. You give a little, and when you receive a little, you then give a little more. Nothing in return? The process stops right there.

It's habitual, even unconscious. People walk around with little warning lights constantly blinking inside: wait . . . wait till you get something in return. After a while, selfless love is a dim memory. It becomes almost impossible to just give. We're so conditioned to the game that doing it any other way is inconceivable.

> Son Owen, just turned seven, hadn't got it yet that you
> ration out your love. He's a bright-eyed little boy. People call
> him Oh. His friend Davey's birthday is approaching. Oh is
> as excited as can be. He loves Davey, you see, and the love is
> still clean.
>
> But a funny thing happens! Oh doesn't get invited to the

party. The day of Davey's birthday comes. Oh can't wait until he talks with Mom. "Let's go to the store right now to buy Davey's present." His eyes are like saucers. Louise's throat catches. "But you haven't been invited to the party." Oh dismisses her comment with a quick curl of his brow that says, What's that have to do with it? She sees he's just a little boy who simply wants to give love to his friend.

They drive to the store, Oh happily picks out the present, and they have it wrapped. When they stop in front of Davey's house, noises of a children's party float from inside. Louise didn't know the party would be going on at that time. Concerned, she glances at the passenger seat. Oh is as excited as ever.

He springs from the car, present in hand, flies up the steps, and rings the bell. Smiling ear to ear, ignoring the noises from inside, he hands the present to Davey's mother. "That's for Davey," he beams. She's speechless. Davey appears at the door. Oh is delighted. He takes the present from the mother and thrusts it into Davey's equally delighted hands. "Gee, thanks," Davey says. Totally pleased, Oh puts his hands in his pockets, turns, and walks off the porch, glowing.

The love here in the Selfless Mountains is like the panting, wriggling, overwhelming love that puppies shower on little children—flagrant exhibitionist love; smiling, touching, happy love. But it's even much more than that; it's far deeper. Love is palpable when it's this pure and simple. There's a wondrous something special that occurs between the giver of it and the receiver of it. It's as though the space between them fills and overflows with this wonder. God knows—and deep inside, puppies and little children also know—what goes on in that space, but only the echoes of it remain in later years.

This is the land of mother's love in the ideal, love at its most charming and sweetest extreme. This love knows not the bounds of convention. No codes of conduct restrict it. This is love from nature, given because it's what you do rather than what you are supposed to do. It is genuine, guileless, uncontrived, simple, spontaneous, innocent love—an impulsive, instinctive love. It's so rare it's priceless, beyond any value a gem could bring.

Why this immense value? Whence this great gift? What's the cosmic secret hovering here? The value comes from one thing: selflessness. There's no *self* in this love (little-*s*, ego self). Either the love is so strong it breaks the usual ties to worldliness, or we learn to occasionally leave the worldly self behind. During times of selflessness we glimpse the peaks where there's an idea even mightier than our ego. That's the magnificence of this place: it connects us with higher forces.

Love as Energy *(Powered Love)*

We're transported into the high peaks country. It's a magical mixture of clarity and mist. There are broad vistas one moment where you experience near total expansion; then suddenly, you turn inward, to the quiet within. As we rise higher, we become aware (as shown here graphically) we're passing through a boundary, moving from the pull of worldly toward the pull of spirit.

We've entered into the invisible, vibrating world of love as a collection of energies. This isn't a form or type of love; love is beyond form here. Love here is pure energy, the energy that drives the various forms of love.

This is Wisdomplace, beyond knowledge; so take care to maintain awareness during this rove through alternating brightness and mist, through intuitive knowing and areas unknowable. Here love reaches out and touches the world and every soul in it. Love here is vibes; it's an invisible movement.

Love at this level drives the new management paradigm; this is the altitude of real leadership, and it is therefore relevant for us to frequent these upper levels. Being open to, and able to draw upon, this energy is a requirement of both superb management and adroit leadership nowadays. Moving closer to this love energy is our audacious mission today.

Love here is will—the power of intentionality. Not a thing moves on the planet without it. Love here is the motive; it's the driver. It's the inner voice (sometimes muffled): "Be loving, love, be loved." Love here is the inclination, the purpose, the urge toward lovingness. It's the primordial direction to feel and be loving.

Love here is ardor. It's the power of eagerness, devotion, and earnestness. It's the power in reaching out and flowing toward others.

Love here is capacity (there's that word again). It refers to fitness, to our worthiness, to whether we have the strength, the sheer amplitude to accept and be receptive. It's having the room inside to allow and to make allowing a way of life. It's the proclivity to welcome in, to embrace. It has to do with one's volume, the margin we have inside for loving. It's of fundamental importance.

And it doesn't stop there. Love here is the goad to grow, the innate sense of moving toward personal improvement. It's a force in every soul on earth now and in all those who ever have been. Growing is life, and it's not easy. The counterpressures toward decay are great, so the force toward growing has to be stronger. And that force is love.

The power of love here is the power of attraction to other beings, not the feelings of attraction or the acts of attracting; rather it's the power itself. It's like magnetism. We can't see or feel it; at times we may think it faint, or even forget about it. But we live with the mysterious pull of love every moment of our existence.

Love here is the primal, soul-deep urge to unity, the high inner knowing that we are one with all others. It's more than identification with others—it's the awareness that on some level we are not separate entities but are all one.

Love here is the summons to wholeness and integrity—the powerful drive toward Source. Love here is the faint inner bidding: "Come home, come home."

Love as Spirit (Being Love)

We lift from the beautiful peaks country into banks of white mist, zooming almost straight upward—quietly, easily. Again we're crossing an invisible boundary, bursting free, as if drawn beyond. After a moment we break over the ridge and soar into a vast quiet. The jagged mountain range is now scarcely a line across the rear horizon. In front, nothingness. No up, no down—limitlessness. No time, no space, just *is*, just beingness.

This is far above and beyond, and yet we feel we've been here before. This is where we came from. This is where love emanates from. There's no movement here even though we're soaring freely. It's so immense we find few words for it: *fundamental, simple, uncomplicated, trusting, expansive, infinite, forever.*

Love here is impersonal—completely, wholly, absolutely unattached, nonneedy—a condition foreign to the worldly mind. And because of that detachment, there's no fear here. None! There's nothing to lose, nothing to gain. That's what's so different here: the fearlessness.

This is where love isn't an attribute or even an energy. It's beyond that; it's more basic, more fundamental. Despite the grand feeling of fearlessness here, we're aware that we're at a seldom-visited level of consciousness, beyond most of our connections to familiar concepts and logic—truly in a new space.

As though to get a bearing, we glance back toward the worldly, squinting into the distance, yet seeing nothing. As we gaze in that direction, however, thin wisps of fear and desire return. So we quickly twist back toward this love/Spirit place; and with that turning, any hint of apprehension fades. We have learned a fundamental lesson: turning away from love weakens; turning toward love (which at this level is the same as turning toward Spirit) is a self-empowering act.

We've come all the way on our mission to love. And now we begin to realize that love is even greater than we had supposed. This is the place where our understanding of the meaning of love begins to coalesce.

This is the place we speak of as Self—higher self or higher consciousness. In this place Spirit and Self are the same. Here, also, is where truth and love are one and the same. And here peace of mind is so great it's beyond worldly quietude; it's an ultimate tranquility, as though peace merges with truth and love and Spirit here. This is where they all swirl, indistinguishable from one another.

Our grasp on the meaning of love grows a bit more firm. This is where the separate strands of love—spirit, self, goodness, source, and so forth—twist together and become a stronger thread. *Is* love all? Poets have proclaimed that over the ages. Our songs say that love is all there is. Could that be?

At first, the idea sounds a bit disconnected—a nice line of poetry, perhaps, or an airy artistic expression. But if we don't let our earthbound thinking hold us—if we turn back toward this level of consciousness and allow the idea to linger in our minds—the possibility that love may be so much more basic than we usually think becomes more imaginable. The ultimate universality of love gradually seems to make some sense.

Is love all? Could love really be everything? If all is love, for example, is love peace? Is it truth? Is it life itself? Is it me? You? Is it *It* indeed? Little by little, the answer seems to flow together, to coalesce: yes! And that affirmative revelation repeats, becoming more defined with each repetition. Yes. Yes, *everything*. The more we live with it, the more it gains essence. Yes. Love really is all, and all is love; indeed, everything at this level is everything else.

Chapter 8

Putting Love to Work

It's time to return to earth and reply more specifically to the Midwest executives (chapter 6) and their concerns about the appropriateness of love in the workplace.

As you recall, they fear being maneuvered into acting lovingly. They don't like the implication that they might have to discard and lay to rest their "nonloving" old selves. They also spoke of the dangers of being labeled weak or weird, of being taken advantage of if they display lovingness on the job. To them, love on the job can be poison or even career suicide. From their angle, being scared is downright logical. If acting more lovingly requires one to toss one's old self, then naturally there will be resistance. As writer Jesse Lair (1985) says, "I may not be much, babe, but I'm all I've got."

ALLOWING LOVE

These executives are also concerned that the cold, hard parts of their jobs— tough decisions, taking charge, enforcing, and so forth—fly in the face of loving, which to them is warm and soft. It's those tough things, after all, that define their tigerness—and that is what they originally signed on for.

Well, they're right! The fact is that rendering love *can* be arsenic or self-destruction. Acting sweet on Mean Street is not smart. And yes, you do bump into tough situations on the job. There are times when you have to be the boss. Some jobs call for a lot of handling of disputes, and you put your gladiators in those jobs. Sometimes, outward niceness is impossible. Sometimes, the job does call for acting like a tiger.

So what can we do? First, let's address the concern about being forced to toss your old self. I flatly state that espousing love does not mean you'll have to trade in you for a shinier model. You've already got everything you need for this lifetime; people come fully equipped, including having an ample supply of lovingness.

To be sure, many people don't feel loving; indeed, there are many who on the surface don't seem to be, and maybe even some who aren't. As a general rule, however, people are loving. Daily, they do little acts that fit under that heading. But they don't see those little acts as loving. They aren't aware they're loving, or they hide it; some direct it to only a thin slice of their lives—for example, toward their kids.

> Like my mother. Subtle love. Lots of cloud covering. Ma felt funny openly expressing it. But it was there. We knew. My father was a successful businessman but he died at the wrong time, leaving a mountain of debt that Ma shouldered for years afterward. So there wasn't much money around the house in our high school years. Yet, every football season Ma scrounged around and found extra money somewhere so that my brothers and I were able to quit our jobs and play on the team. That was loving, with not a word spoken—and sometimes there was a bit of groaning—yet we all knew love was happening; we just didn't call it by name.

Turn back a few pages in your mind to what loving means. It means reverence: politeness, caring, and respect. Now we've all experienced that—even on the job. It also means feelings: sentiments like affection, attraction, trust, liking, sympathy. It means action: deeds of friendliness, helping out, sharing, welcoming, and so forth. We all feel and do those things; we just don't include them in the love column when we add it up.

Why don't we? Maybe we're wary of the taint of desire that's in all love on a worldly level. We sense that slight imperfection and think the good we're doing isn't pure, and thus isn't good. But that taint isn't bad; it just *is*. At this worldly level, all good has a fleck of bad in it, just as all bad has a speck of good in it. Yet, for some reason, we don't allow our goodness. We have to learn to appreciate our good deeds and chalk them up in the love column even if we keep the ledger to ourselves.

> Doug was the chief executive of a large organization that was in the middle of a massive employee involvement program. The company's one hundred key executives just sat through a grueling day of honest, almost-blunt reports from groups of employees.
>
> He and I and a couple of these executives had dinner together that evening. It was a long, lonely, and difficult meal since they were still chewing on the feedback that had been stuffed in them all afternoon. After dinner Doug circled back to the hotel meeting room.
>
> There he was, at 11:45 P.M., a lonely figure in a huge, mostly dark room, sitting cross-legged on the floor amidst piles of papers, poring over the unedited raw data presented that day by the working folks.
>
> Word of this spread quickly. At breakfast the next morning every one of the participants had heard that the boss cared (that is, loved) enough to burn the midnight oil.
>
> The signal was clear: listen, pay attention, care! As the key executives attending the conference worked at that, organizational priorities shifted. The program was eventually a big success. They didn't call it love, but inwardly they knew.

Even the high mountains of selfless love aren't as distant as people think. No-strings love shows up sooner or later in everyone's life. For example, when loved ones are ill, people take care of them with hardly a second thought. They just care, and they don't expect a cake for it. That giving and caring is what we're talking about. That's selflessness. We need to be aware of it, to treasure it.

Love *is* in all our lives! It's all around us. It's near at hand whether or not we reach out and touch it. We can decide not to be like Bill, the stoic Brit who repeatedly spoke of his closed heart. His heart wasn't closed and neither are any of ours. In fact, at the place beyond the peaks, in the quiet, misty realm of love as Spirit, we *are* love, as we recall, swirling together as in a cosmic dance—not two separate things, one.

But here, back in the world, we do more acting than dancing. While our part may not call for open demonstrations of it, love is written into all the characters we play. There's shy love and subtle love, just as there is open love, demonstrative, and huggy love. There's even cranky love. There are as many kinds of love as there are people. Each of us is a loving being in his or her own way.

It turns out that this old self will do, after all, because love is indeed very much a part of it.

RELEVANT LOVE

Now we tackle the other key question posed by the group of executives: is love relevant in the business world? If we answer from our lower (bodily/worldly) selves, we don't know. From that depressed angle, we see the tigers roaming the mean streets. It's fearful down there. But if we answer from our higher selves, our reply is instantaneous: certainly love is relevant! No doubt about it. Since there's little fear in higher self, love comes easily.

So the real answer to this crucial question—whether love is relevant in the business world—is: it depends. If we come only from our under selves, where fear resides and there's not as much room for love, then, the answer is: perhaps not. If, on the other hand, we come from our higher selves, where there's very little room for fear, the answer is: certainly! Love and fear do not coexist well. Adding higher self, which means adding Spirit and love to our consciousness, uplifts and strengthens us.

Love Goes to Work

What are the implications of all this on the job? We must, after all, fulfill our trust at work. We have to meet our obligations as well as we can. We owe it to ourselves to do our utmost best in this world.

That means we must do all those hard things like being the boss, laying down the law, making "tough" decisions, whatever is required. But we mustn't forget our spiritual dimension; we must do those things with an eye toward that other aspect of ourselves, doing them from love rather than fear.

Look at it from the perspective of success on the job. In work, the object is to accomplish. "Work" means digging in and getting things done. But accomplishment in organizations is always achieved through other human beings. You're constantly, invariably working with people, whether you're at their level, above them, or below them.

Working well through others requires cooperation, teamwork, loyalty, understanding, tolerance, helping, unity, and amity. It calls for trust, caring, helping, enabling, empowering. And what are these? They're not just the essentials of work effectiveness, they're qualities of love! Love isn't just nice—it's imperative. Recall the furrow-browed executives who so immediately answered in the affirmative about reverence in their best-ever relationships at work (chapter 4). They weren't just being nice. They were acknowledging this great force.

Love at work is beyond softness and niceness. It includes whether people really respect and care about one another, whether they reach out and help, whether they protect one another's dignity, and whether they give without (too many) strings attached. Those are loving qualities in action.

The reality of this world is that we have to be effective within the system. To do that well, we have to be loving, and our loving must be strong. Dump the idea that love has to be soft. Real love can be hard or soft. Sure, maybe you're a gruff general. I've met many. But I've met loving gruff generals and despicable gruff generals. Doug, the chief who burned the midnight oil, was a tough boss *and* loving man. It was Doug's caring that provided the extra jot of energy that roused his colleagues and brought success. He wasn't especially warm, but he came from love.

We can't blame the job for lack of loving. The problem is not that job roles don't have love in them; in fact, they're neutral. It's that people are performing the roles in a nonloving way. It's a matter of the backdrop we create, against which we play out our life. Is it love or fear? Sure, in certain situations it may be harder to come from love; but, as stated above, there are only two choices: love or fear.

We hold that in mind while we return, as promised, to Isaac and the Hard Rock Cafe. When we left this young executive, he was flying around the globe tending his restaurant flock. As his life thread spins out, he's pretty sure he's doing it right, although he doesn't really know . . .

"What Is Your Way?"

Isaac's India connection continues but in a peculiar way.
Once or twice a year he travels there for a fortnight. His brisk
life-style halts while he sits and muses, seeking the holy man's
blessing and guidance. Yet it never comes—directly. Year
after year for fifteen years the thread spins, bringing life's

inevitable highs and lows. Isaac is growing all the while, his life convictions thickening and mellowing.

Thousands of times he asks, "Am I on the right track?" But he never gets to talk personally with Sai Baba. His answers have to come from within. He increasingly learns to look inside, and the love that dwells in that space carries over into his business.

All he knows for sure is that things are going well. The restaurant's success can't be contained. Over the years the company opens several more restaurants in leading world cities like New York, Tokyo, and Stockholm. Later the business expands even more through a sister company. Times change, especially in the restaurant business, and Isaac's strategies take the company into the far-different eighties and then into the even more dissimilar nineties. The Hard Rock Cafe clothing line becomes a more important part of it. Business continues to boom.

On all company paychecks various aphorisms of love are printed. In every restaurant kitchen in big brass letters is "Love all, serve all." On one wall of every restaurant is a large photo of Sai Baba. Patrons look, blink, stop chewing, and ask, "Who's that?" "We call it the God wall" is the reply. "Oh," the patrons mumble, and chew on that for a while.

Isaac closely protects the basic concept of friendly classlessness and guards the organization's values. In the various cultures his businesses enter, it's not easy. His primary stratagem is to create a friendly, loving, status-free climate within each staff. And that's not easy either.

"In Tokyo," he says, "we had to train people not to bow—unheard of in Japan! And we insisted that women, who are nonentities there, be treated absolutely equally. In Stockholm, we couldn't get our waitresses to flash a smile and approach people in a friendly way. The Swedes may be quiet and proper, but they're also nice people, so how come? I started asking people. About half the waitresses finally admitted they were reluctant because in Sweden people think you're drunk if you act that way. We eventually worked it out. Now it's the most successful restaurant in the city," Isaac says, "as are all of our restaurants in each of our cities."

He switches the subject to the spirit behind his endeavors. "All I did," he reflects, "is put spirit and business together in that big mixing bowl and add love. I didn't care about anything but the people. Just cherish them, look after them, be sensitive to them and their lives." The reverence he feels shines through his blue eyes. "That important relationship with my staff is what made the Hard Rock, nothing else! It was an opportunity to blend spiritual life and business life."

All this is reflected in the selling price, an unheard-of value in that industry. Why did he sell? "Oh, I finished that karma. It's time to move on, plus the world changed," he says seriously. "But we did set things straight, b'god—and isn't that what dharma is all about?"

Weeks later, walking down the street, I hear someone hail me. It's Isaac! We exchange greetings and he says, "Sai Baba finally took me in for a personal talk!" "Great," I say, eager to hear more. Isaac tells me the story.

He and six others were invited into Baba's private interview room. At the start of the meeting, Baba looked from one person to the next, asking about each one's spiritual path. "And how do you go toward Truth, sir?" Then he'd move on to the next, "And what is your way, madam?" And so on, around the room.

"I was last in line," Isaac breathes. "As the others talked, I mentally rehearsed my answers; I didn't want to blow it after waiting so long. Finally Baba got to me . . . but he didn't ask the question!" Isaac pauses, sighs. "He just leaned over, put his face close, smiled, and said, 'Love all, serve all.'"

In a subdued voice Isaac continues, "It was a confirmation of nineteen years of hard work." We both stand quietly in the busy street for a few moments. He glances up, then at me; there's just a slight hint of that outraged teenager in his eyes. "Y'know, there are other things for me to do in this world." We shake hands warmly, promise to meet again, and walk our separate ways.

So we meet and face the question a final time: *is* love relevant at work? And again the answer: yes. It's even crucial. It has to be an expanded genus of love, one that does not brand you odd or soft. Whether hard or soft, it does have to be there. People know in a nanosecond when love isn't home.

PART III

REPOWERING

REALIGNING BELIEFS, THOUGHTS, AND BEING

This section puts five powerful notions to work: (1) *belief* is the basic foundation of our being; (2) *thought power* can shape our very lives; (3) *already-thereness* is a way to leap to our next level; (4) *instantaneousness* posits that deep change can, and often does, sweep quickly over human systems; and (5) *untethering* from worldly "stuff" is the way to freedom.

79

CHAPTER 9

THE POWER OF BELIEFS AND THOUGHTS

Sooner or later when dealing with character and spirit, you run smack into the matter of belief. Why? Because belief is the bedrock, the bottom element of it. Belief is faith; belief is confidence and trust. Belief is not only the foundation of spirituality, but also it's the basis of character, management, and organization. Without basic belief these structures wobble.

BELIEF MATTERS

What a great idea—belief. Belief as the stupendous force that shapes us and molds our character and our organizations' character. Thus, if we clarify and redirect our basic beliefs, we can reshape life itself! Okay, but belief in what? Belief in self as part of something greater, belief in a goodness that forms integrity—and, as we will see, belief in belief itself.

Dr. Roger Sperry (1991) of Caltech, the Nobel laureate who sorted out the various right- and left-brain specialties, says that "as a brain scientist [he] considers belief to be the force which *above any other* shapes the course of human affairs." (Emphasis his.)

At a workshop on mind-body control, Tony demonstrates a
way to help a person switch mental states, for example, how
to flip from dourness to delight. Obviously a practical tool.

81

We pair up to try it on one another. I go first. I do and say exactly what he had demonstrated . . . but it doesn't work.

"How come it worked for you and not me?" He looks at me and shifts from light banter to serious teaching. "I believe I can do it, you don't," he says.

I feel a blink of defensiveness, and then realization: he's right. He believes he can and, at this point, I don't. That's the difference between success or failure here. I sit quietly for a while in the light of this learning, fascinated with this small encounter with the might of belief. It is so simple it almost gets away from you, and yet it's so powerful.

Belief—conviction, knowing, faith, trust, confidence, whatever you call it—is the force that conveys to us our essence. Call it something that does it justice: brawny belief, belief from the heart, belief at the level of being, belief from the realm of self—higher self.

This is belief far beyond the intellect's unsteady reach for logic and proof. This belief opens the way for inner truth; it steadies and assures, it brings the silent roar of inner conviction. This is ballast-for-life believing. It's cosmic belief. It's believing so large that it envelops and sweeps us along with it; a belief so deep that it shades into real knowing, which ultimately, as we will see, is faith.

Always, at the very base of a human system's culture are the beliefs it holds. This is true whether it's one's personal culture, an organization's culture, or a society's.

BELIEF AND BODY

We know that belief performs apparently magical healing of the physical body. Miraculous remissions come not through pills but through some force within us connected to our believing processes. We know that a mysterious transformation of energy takes place that brings health. Hmm. And we know that this energy issues from the strength of belief. Some people seem more endowed with this power than others, but we know it's in all of us.

Harvard researcher Herb Benson's (1975) first book, *The Relaxation Response*, focused on the body's capacity, through becoming quiet, to reduce heart and breathing rates, metabolism, and blood pressure. These were hitherto believed to be impossible to consciously control.

Still fascinated, however, the good doctor pushed deeper into the getting-well process. He had to journey far afield, literally. At one point, his research took him to the Himalayas to investigate the unbelievable ability of some Tibetan monks to drastically alter their body temperature up to 15 degrees Fahrenheit above normal. They do this while in deep meditation, apparently through some mental (or beyond mental) process associated with the belief that they can do it.

Tibet, however, was a side trip. Benson's real exploration was inner. He burrowed into the observable phenomena connected with the role that belief plays in healing. This Bostonian doctor-professor found something at the core of the getting-well process that seems quite far from hard science: faith!

Benson's (1987a) second book, *Beyond the Relaxation Response*, features the "faith factor." In this book Benson hangs out a laundry list of things that believing can do: relieve headaches, reduce angina pains, lower blood pressure, enhance creativity, ease backaches, overcome insomnia, prevent panic attacks, lower cholesterol levels, enhance cancer therapy. That's just a sampling—there are many more.

According to his research, believing comes and heals in something like 75 percent of all illnesses. The physicians I've worked with readily agree and even revise the figure up to 90 percent or more. You thought it was capsules that made you well? It is belief that summons the cure.

Benson found something even more fascinating: belief itself is healthy. According to him, just possessing a strong belief is the healing force. His measured research showed that when people believe in something, regardless of what, they're healthier. It's not what you believe in but the state of belief itself that does the healing! Believing is what's crucial.

This is a strikingly relevant point. We're back at page one, running smack into the matter of belief. And again the question is, belief in what? Well, at the very core it's a primordial confidence, a basic trust that there is a greater hand than ours at work in our lives. It's a basic belief in belief, which is really our belief in a power outside of our comprehension.

This force may be beyond us or within us. It may be something we tap into, or it may be something that we already have—or are. Whatever it is and wherever it is located, we know it exists. Research is again confirming what we already know: that there's a stupendous power within our purview that stems from our beliefs.

The Doers

There are legions of people who use this force; some are sometimes called healers. Whether amateur or professional, they're people with good hearts and hot hands, ready to help others connect to their inner healing powers.

There are, of course, thousands of healing stories floating around. We've all heard many of these stories from around the planet and from all walks of life. Here's a close-to-home example from Southern California and the ashram (I use it because of the drama in it, not to imply that this is the only way).

Linda tells me the delivery room staff became grave during the birth of her son. Crestfallen, they turned to her and asked, "Should we baptize the baby?" She didn't know quite what to think. Within the next few days it becomes clear that little Parker's toehold in the world is scant indeed. Born prematurely and hydrocephalic, the two-pound body undergoes his first operation within a few hours of birth: a new valve is stitched into the tiny beating heart.

The next three months are an unending series of life-and-death struggles, but Parker hangs on. The tiny body is all but buried beneath life-support hook-ups and monitors. Frequent CAT scans follow the progress of the "bleed" into his head.

During that time, Linda's and Howard's friends and relatives pray for the little boy. Someone gives Linda a small packet of *vibhuti* (the sacred ash that comes from Sai Baba's fingers), hoping it might help. A photograph of this little human connected to myriad tubes, bottles, and machines is taken to Baba in India. Baba comments, "He [Parker] hasn't decided whether he wants to stay here." A few weeks later Baba says, "Tell the mother he will be all right." Linda and Howard take heart.

In the third month, however, the doctors, more grave than usual, inform the parents that the bleed isn't improving and a shunt (brain surgery) is imperative. They had been holding off to see if the prayers would work, but they can't wait any longer. The operation is scheduled for the next day.

That night the young parents steal into the intensive care unit. In the semidarkness they gently rub the *vibhuti* over the tiny chest and onto their son's head. Then Linda touches a spot of ash to Parker's forehead. "Please, Baba, a miracle," she pleads.

In the morning the phone rings. "Hello, Linda, this is the doctor (breathless pause) . . . we can't understand it . . . the bleed arrested, we won't have to do the shunt." Linda slumps to the floor, shoulders shaking. Howard runs over, grabs her and the phone, and hears the doctor's happy news. They sit, holding each other, as deep, wracking sobs of relief roll over them. At that instant the Kenny Loggins song line "This is your miracle" plays over the radio.

It's not over yet though. There are many other difficulties. Parker's breathing problems, for example, continue and later require emergency surgery. Linda tells me, "Looking back, it seems as though I spent the first full year of Parker's life sitting with him in a La-Z-Boy chair." The doctors, nurses, and social workers all gravely inform Linda and Howard of the inevitable learning disabilities and other potential problems.

A few years later, when it's clear that the happy little boy is going to be normal in every way, one of the social workers shakes her head, "This is an example of the power of faith and love." (They're both the same when you get to the high-faith level.) Parker is a radiant six-year-old the first time I meet him.

Sai Baba, who is apparently one of the vortices of these healing powers, says, "There are no 'healers.' All healing comes from connecting with the Power that heals." Recall the vignette in the introduction about the young women who asked Baba to heal their friend of cancer, and he replied, "But where is the capacity?" Capacity again. Belief is a large part of capacity.

Belief, relative to physical health, is important and dramatic; but health is just one aspect of this power. According to Dr. Sperry (1991), remember, belief is the force that shapes *all* human affairs!

BELIEF IN ORGANIZATIONS

Does belief power also hold for organizations of humans? Sure. We all know of, and have been part of, various organizations: some do and some don't believe in themselves.

The high-tech subsidiary, call it 3C, of a major automaker is located in a nice campus setting; nevertheless, there's a general seething there. Missed delivery dates, missing morale, and messy quality problems are menacing them. They haven't seen a profit in five years and, because of that, have seen four new top managers during that time. Relationships with the parent company aren't anything to write home, or the home office, about.

But it's not the relationship outside, it's the one inside that aches. People at 3C have been called losers so often they're starting to believe it. They feel hurt, insulted, and scared that it may be true. Worse yet, everything the organization touches seems to be fulfilling these base beliefs. Even the products (communications satellites) aren't working right.

But they aren't really losers. The high-tech industry is full of bright people and those at 3C are at least as good as the rest. They're well-thought-of outside, but at home, zilch. It all feels so unjust and so wrong.

The new CEO, Roy, is a seasoned pro. He's competent, he's a nice guy—and he's manipulative, political, nervous, and under great pressure to perform. He brings in the consultants at the subtle insistence of corporate HQ. He's got a can of worms in his hands and does not know how to handle it. They want him to initiate an employee involvement program, which to him feels like a plot to pop the lid off the can.

Thus, the getting-started phase is almost the snuffing-out phase. Roy is Mr. Caution, afraid that one bad move gets him tossed onto the predecessor heap. Plans are written, rewritten, and then re-rewritten. Meetings are piled on meetings, presentations on presentations. It's costing the company a bundle and the consultants their patience. The atmosphere calls for a graceful exit of the consultants, but they reach into reserves for patience they didn't know they had and hang on.

Slowly—with lots of clanging and banging—a program plan is hammered out. The aim: rejuvenate the climate and bring back self-confidence. The latest plan is about the same as the original proposal except for some cosmetics to make it look okay to the parent company. The general strategy is to involve large numbers of employees, sowing seeds widely with the hope that some will flower later.

Over the ensuing months everyone in the organization is asked the question, How are we going to turn this thing around? The responses—unvarnished, unedited, and uncomfortable—are bundled into a report. It's a doozer! They make sure HQ doesn't see it for a while.

In the first phase, all 125 managers begin working on the issues identified in the report. Threaded throughout this phase are meetings in which they talk about basic purpose and meaning. Managers are given special care and attention—private briefings, a series of Management Community Conferences, bimonthly Dinner Workshops, and so forth. Referring to them as a management community brings jeers at first; however, that label provides a healthier way of thinking about themselves and the idea slowly permeates the atmosphere.

The publicly stated agenda in the sessions is to "work problems." The private agenda consists of catharsis, massaging hurts, and coming around to the truth—the central message of the whole program: *we are okay!*

The second phase is similar but done with rank-and-file workers. Many of the better managers join with the consultants to institute study groups, committees, quality circles, task forces, and such. The emphasis once more is on widespread participation in problem solving; again, there's an opportunity to discuss purpose and meaning. As all this happens, the same truth gradually works its way through to everybody: *we are okay!*

That message takes hold in the spare soil and grows: *we really are okay!* With their self-esteem reawakened, the downward slide bottoms out. Everything seems to improve; even the satellites begin to work better.

Again it's a respiriting, but this time with an emphasis on *rebelieving* in themselves. A little wobbly maybe, but nonetheless true. It takes a year. It becomes clear that the extra

patience during the getting-started phase came from the
belief that the ripped-away spirit hadn't been killed and
would return as their belief in themselves came home.

We've often heard the notion, "What we believe, we are." At first, it sounds nonsensical, as though the sentence didn't get finished. The implications, however, are profound. If a person believes a certain way about himself, he will be that way—and vice versa: if he doesn't believe, he won't be that way. The same holds for beliefs about the world. "The loving man lives in a loving world, the hostile man lives in a hostile world," goes the saying.

Could that really be true? Is belief really so consequential in our lives? What part do our thoughts play in all this?

RIGHT THINKING

> *Thoughts so strong they act as*
> *beliefs, and beliefs strong enough*
> *to make things happen.*
> —J. H.

As we know, there's a definite connection between our thoughts, our beliefs, and our spirit. Let's veer into an apparent sidestream of belief: thoughts. There is much ado nowadays regarding the power of thought. Many techniques for shaping thinking—and thus our moods, perceptions, and basic experience of life—have surfaced over the past few years. There's great excitement and potential in it.

We need to pay much attention to training the mind. In our minds are both hurtful and helpful thoughts. Like with beliefs, the trick is to make sure that our thoughts are right for us, not wrong. It is of utmost importance that we play the right ones: thoughts that cheer, that nourish; vitamins-for-the-soul thoughts; thoughts that move us upward, closer to Spirit.

There are various right-thought approaches. Some practitioners say to let go of negative thoughts. Others instruct to accept them and then move on. Others direct that nothing but good thoughts be allowed into the mind in order to leave absolutely no room for negatives. And still others enjoin us to perfect our language, choosing to drop from our vocabulary all words of negativity, criticism, fear, sarcasm, and the like. The idea here is that negative moods flourish through the use of words, that we "language" ourselves into darkness. Each approach has its own set of techniques that work.

My friend Gary, a lifelong, competitive tennis player, tells how over a three-year period he improved his won-lost record by 70 percent and ended up capturing the club championship. His tennis regimen (borrowed from his spiritual growth efforts)mainly included rigorous thought training. He taught himself to never, that's never *ever,* think a negative thought—whether about his opponent or himself, or anyone or anything. This applied to the periods before, during, and after his matches.

He became so sensitive to this he could immediately feel his body strain when even the most minor negative moved in. This good thinking went leagues beyond the grudging handshake at the net; he trained himself to truly think well of his opponents and to flood his mind with happy thoughts when they made a good play or won the match. By the way, not only his game blossomed, his whole life did.

Whatever method we use, the message is again clear: if thoughts really are a force in ordering our worldly lives and our spiritual selves, we'd better be good at thinking. If we really are what we think, then the aim is to think good thoughts, and to keep working at it until there's virtually nothing but good in our heads. Think happy, think win, think health, think higher self—and those characteristics will adhere to your life.

It's not just athletes who do the thought shuffle. Thoughts, even though they may be of heavy importance, are nevertheless rather light; they can be rearranged. As with Benson's (1975, 1987a) relaxation response, right-think is learnable. Shifting to good thoughts can be done without too much effort.

At the beginning of a management team's annual retreat, team members are asked, How's your spirit? It's not a common question, but they've been together for years and have learned the value of eliciting thoughts that shift them above the din for a while.

They take a few moments to think. Fran, one of the staff directors, speaks first. He chats informally about nothing special, small talk about life experiences since the last retreat. Then, his thoughts turn to his son in Little League baseball and his voice shifts.

His words take on a smile as his thoughts convey him to the baseball diamond. "You should see him," he says. "He's a skinny little guy, not very coordinated, sort of shy." He pauses for several moments, tears well up as he becomes aware of his deep love for his son. He quietly adds, "But he has a great heart; he tries so hard." The others slide into an accepting silence, as Fran's thought-borne tenderness triggers their own reveries.

The others continue the discussion, sharing similar "little" experiences from their own lives. In due time they settle into a thoughtful pattern of discussing the work agenda. The conversation is rich and forthright; there's a ring of aliveness and reality in it. It is their thoughts that shape the quality of this work. A penny for your thoughts? Worth much more.

POWER THINKING

As felt, so fashioned.
—Sanskrit proverb

Notwithstanding Ma's quiet loving (chapter 8), there was almost no cheer in her days. Her thoughts carved unhappiness deeply into her soul. The business debt my father left was only one mountain to her. She lived in a whole range of them: the Lousylife Mountains. She seemed almost comfortable there, not cozy, but more like the resignation that comes when you're familiar with a certain pattern of thinking, good or bad.

In Ma's case it wasn't just thinking about negative experiences from days gone by, it was reliving every heartbeat of past dread. She called up the scripts from the dusty archives of her life. They weren't mere memories, they were vivid vignettes in full technicolor with background music. And these mind tapes never wore out; instead, they magically seemed to gain strength and intensity as she aged. After a while Ma just couldn't think any other way.

Hers was a textbook case on thought power, and we can learn from it. Not only did she repeatedly think those memories, but also she heard them, talked them, saw them in her mind's eye, felt them to the marrow in her bones, and probably even smelled and tasted them. It was total sensory involvement.

And that, according to the people who do thought training, is precisely what it takes to fashion thoughts. What Ma did with negative thoughts, we can do with right thoughts. We can use the same mechanisms to repeatedly create positive inner experiences for our own good. We can constantly see, hear, and feel the good things that move us upward, that help us live a gratifying, successful life.

We can choose light. We can decide to step out from the shade into the sun. We can weave positive thoughts into such a tight pattern that they block out darkness. This doesn't mean we attempt to stifle negatives; more so, it's being aware of them, learning whatever there is to learn from them, and then choosing to spin on our heel and walk away from them.

We can comb good thoughts and put them to work for us. Rather than letting our thoughts steal our vigor, we can pick thoughts that nourish. We can even piece together a personal history from positive memories—erasing past errors whose memories weaken us in the present—so that looking back brings strength to our present. This conjured-up strength is just as real as all the personal weaknesses people so often recall, and it's far better for us.

In fact, it is within our power to invite in no less than the most sought after thing on the planet: peace of mind. Inner peace, after all, arises where our thoughts begin, and it extends outward from there.

This kind of thinking isn't just thinking; it's power thinking. The process goes like this: first, choose the (good and right) thoughts we want to be influenced by and add to them the energy and intensity of vision, sound, and emotion. Then, constantly, obsessively repeat those thoughts until they, like beliefs, exert great power in our lives, making good things and right things happen.

If right thinking is so easy, why don't we do it? We don't because we don't believe we can. Somewhere along the way doubt, which is the great enemy of belief, crept in. "Not me, I can't"—while the thought tape autoreverses countless thousands of repetitions, below the level of consciousness, until "can't" becomes belief. One of the main tasks while on the spiritual path is to gradually repeal all of these wrong beliefs and thoughts.

As I write this, I suddenly notice we've slipped from talking about thoughts back to talking about beliefs. It seems they're but different aspects of the same thing. We're abruptly back from the trip up the "tributary," only to find it was circular. Thought, then, isn't a sidestream of belief; rather, it's part of the main river that circled around and returned to itself.

CHAPTER 10

HIGH BELIEF AND MOMENTS OF FAITH

Many of the currently popular techniques for shaping thoughts and beliefs are exciting. We desperately want to accept that we can do it all, that all this power can accrue to us. The idea is so beguiling: great believing makes a great me!

Too fat? Think thin, or buy a cassette tape that helps you think thin. Tennis stroke cobwebby? Swing into Zen tennis. Shy? Befriend a tape that continuously affirms your warm, outgoing nature. Et cetera. There are thousands of applications of the technology of belief.

Some are great fun; they're entertaining, they're serious. And the outcomes are often astounding. People *do* look better, feel better, stroke better, and all that.

Yet my writer friend Pat, sitting with one foot in the River Belief, is sort of crestfallen. There's a faraway look on her face. "I want to believe in thought power and affirmations and such," she says, her eyes drifting upward, "but, well, it doesn't work for me." Her honesty splashes cool water from the river. I'm again reminded that it may be simple, but it's not easy. No warranties come with thought- and belief-training techniques. They aren't "products" that can simply be plucked off the shelf.

BELIEVEURISM

You can't just grab for the outcomes of believing without going to the trouble of actually believing. That's like trying to get the benefit of illumination without putting batteries in the flashlight, or like concentrating on the harvest at the expense of the sowing, watering, weeding, and caring required along the way. It's a fixation on yield without considering the investment.

If we could magically go into this phenomenon of belief as we did with spirit (chapter 3), we would again see the rock with wavy lines emanating from it. This time the rock would be labeled "B" for beliefs and the squiggly lines raying out from it would be the force of belief.

The lines depict the energy of belief; they reach out and bring about the results we know come from believing. But remember, they aren't belief, they simply indicate its power. Many people, without thinking of it, have become *believeurs;* they go after the squiggles and forget the bedrock. It doesn't really work without both, and even then it might not work.

Belief is as much something we *are* as something we do. It's a state of mind, a way of being. We've got to *be* the rock—being this believing—and then the wavy lines come. Maybe at the entry level it's something we do, sort of like rehearsing; but beyond that, one doesn't "do" believing, one has it or is it.

Belief is the basis for doing, not the actual doing. It's the power behind (or above) the feat rather than the accomplishment of it. They may seem interchangeable, and in some cases they appear to be, but you've got to have both aspects. You can't consistently put something into effect if you don't have it in the first place.

The very source of belief is in Spirit, deep within. Yet people, in the grip of a materially oriented, "worldly" world, unthinkingly treat belief power as another commodity that can be bought, something to be exploited for worldly gain. If we see belief as a spiritual rather than as a worldly phenomenon, we won't do that.

We have to remember, too, that not everything we want to realize or actualize through positive beliefs is right for us to realize or actualize. That's why Tibetan teachers, who are *the* masters of this, seldom aim to actualize anything specific. Instead, it's better to surrender to a higher will (to that source of belief—Spirit—within), trusting it to provide what's appropriate.

Let's again use an illustrative story from the ashram to help get across some of this.

It is Michael's first visit to India. On the list of things for this smiling, vigorous young man to see is the famous holy man, Sai Baba. Meanwhile it is the last visit for Don, who over the past twenty years has conducted some twenty tour groups from the States to see Baba. This time, Don's vigor is gone, his speech is slurred, his body is obviously gravely ill. It's as if Don has quietly come home for the last time.

Michael, interested, curious, settles into the ashram routine. After several peaceful days, he decides to bring his favorite crystal, a clear, medium-blue beauty, to morning *darshan* (when Baba comes out to be with the people), hoping that Baba will bless it. That day, as he usually does at *darshan*, Baba slowly works his way around the large crowd. Michael is sitting a few paces to my right, Don is sitting to my left. Baba slowly glides through the throng, stopping here and there to talk to someone or listen to someone's plaints. He occasionally produces a small gift, a laugh, or a tear. Everyone's eyes are intently on him as he proceeds toward where we are sitting.

Michael, holding his breath, holds out the clear stone for the blessing. Baba stops, looks at the stone, looks at Michael, glances back at the stone and then back at Michael. He raises his eyebrows and his head comes forward slightly to add emphasis to what he's about to say. "Madness," he intones, then moves on. The single word comes as an instruction, not a rebuke.

Baba walks over to Don and motions for him to go into the inner room for a private interview. Some minutes later Don emerges and makes his way back toward his seat, a broad grin on his gray face. He flashes a victory wink and holds up a clear glass, or crystal, lingam (an egg-shaped object often associated with physical health), which Baba had presented to him.

Don, very happy with the gift, is deeply grateful. Baba is reminding him to believe in the core truth that the real him is not the shriveled body, that his Spirit remains untouched by this illness. A few days later he peacefully leaves his body.

For Michael it's a beginning, not an end. After *darshan*, we stop and talk. He, too, is grateful for his encounter with Baba, knowing he also got a gift, but he isn't yet sure what it is.

I'm fascinated by the two crystalline gifts. One is "madness," the other a symbolic trinket. Both, I'm sure, are profound boons.

About a week later Michael, beaming, stops me in the street. "Hey, I figured it out, it's a great teaching: Baba is telling me not to put my belief in *any*thing outside myself!"

MANAGEMENT BELIEF

There is also *believeurism* in management nowadays. Much that comes under the heading of leadership visioning and strategic imaging, for example, is not solidly based in real belief. Well-intentioned though it may be, often it's but flying leaps at the wavy lines, attempts to exploit the power of belief without considering the bedrock of it. Without real belief, the leaps fall short.

A year ago, colleague Charles and I are talking about visioning in management and about how the literature continues to harp the need for "leadership vision." We exchange our experiences with many of the currently popular techniques for clarifying vision. Some work, some don't; there's something missing. Charles, a veteran consultant, slumps his shoulders in defeat. "Visioning is a pretty horse you can't ride," he sighs. He's referring to vision the commodity, the product.

Yet we know that vision based on faith is powerful; it heals, and it can mobilize people to action. Vision based on faith?—faith in what? The answer is circular (again). It's faith in the power of faith! Your vision must contain a belief in the power of vision for it to work. Tricky.

Consultant-author Peter Block (1987) writes of the despondency experienced by managers in strategic-visioning programs. After they're through the bow wave of hope, they start to put action steps and delivery dates onto their exciting visions and—plop—the whole thing goes flat. Why? It's hard to translate dreams into real life. They begin to see into a sweaty future that's just the same old stuff sporting a few new labels.

We see so many managers, good people, shuffling along in the ongoing parade of "Programs": Total Quality Management (TQM), Quality of Worklife (QWL), Employee Involvement (EI), whatever. They're high-level people, adults, dutifully going through the motions, following orders to be committed to this or that program.

They try to talk themselves into believing in it; to an extent it may work, but more often it doesn't. Being managers, they are for the most part well-intentioned—and they're also seasoned manipulators. It's hard for them not to fall for the ol' forced-commitment ploy because they've used it so many times themselves.

Thus, the ongoing parade of capital-letter Programs continues. And the sham committed managers continue their parade shuffle. It's a costly march—costly in dollars and time, and costly in integrity, which is priceless.

To be fair to the trudging managers, getting into the march does sometimes work. The tactic of just going with it—"faking it till you're making it"—can, and sometimes does, succeed. Oftentimes the march itself may be good exercise, the process itself helping nudge the system closer to health.

Apparently some measure of—that is, "enough" belief—is needed even if it's not 100 percent. Expecting total belief every time would be oppressive. How much is "enough" belief? You have to go inside yourself for the answer.

EXPECTATIONS AND BELIEF

Expectations call on the same deep power as belief. What we really expect, we get. Expect the best and chances are you'll get it. Expect the worst: ditto.

Researcher Albert King (1974) tells of controlled experiments with the mysterious power of top-management expectations. The president of a company instituted certain changes in work procedures at four of the company's plants. He tells the managers of plants A and C that he expects the new ways of doing things to raise productivity but not morale; he tells the managers of plants B and D that he expects the improvements to boost morale but not productivity.

You guessed it. A's and C's productivity shoots up, but their measures of morale (absenteeism, turnover, grievances, and so on) show no variance; the workers in plants B and D grow happier, but production stays where it was! The power of boss expectations is truly startling.

Similarly startling are the often-reported classroom experiments where researchers tested the impact of teacher expectations on the learning success of the pupils. Classes composed of students of similar capabilities are used in the experiments, but teachers are told that certain classes are quick learners and others are slow.

You guessed it again. The results are disconcerting: classes labeled bright do beautifully, the ones labeled dull, dismally. It is the teachers' *expectations*, not the abilities of the students, that bring the results.

Another example is the Army. This huge, supposedly rigid bureaucracy is well aware of the magic in expectations and has developed a successful way to apply it. The Army systematically clarifies boss beliefs and expectations through a training module known as Transition of Command.

Deceptively simple, a Transition of Command session has the new boss get together with those who report directly to him to discuss basic beliefs and expectations in the context of the organization's short-term goals. A set of information requests shapes the agenda (this is what we need to know about you, here's what you need to know about us, these are our priorities over the next several months, and so on). A facilitator helps them.

Why do this? The military faces the same disruption, confusion, and loss of productivity as other organizations do when leadership changes. They carry out this process to help new commanders land running.

New bosses appreciate doing it, and subordinates like hearing it. The process builds understanding and trust, which is the basis of boss credibility. The model works so well it has caught on down to company commander transitions. The U.S. Forest Service heard of it and put it to use; it spread like, excuse the expression, wildfire. A transition session is now routine when new managers take over.

This uncomplicated model builds trust because expectations and beliefs are laid out so straight. Bosses' credibility goes up as their basic beliefs and expectations—like them or not—come out in the open. People know what's important to the new boss and can deal with him or her accordingly. It's just good, commonsense management, making good use of the magic of belief.

BELIEF AND SPIRIT

So we return again: beliefs do matter. We repeatedly learn that believing is at the heart of things. Take spirit, even. You want to know where meaning, purpose, and inspiration come from? Belief! Believing is authority, bedrock, and support base. It's the source of dedication, the very basis of commitment.

Belief is at the very heart of everything we've talked about or will be talking about in this book. From one angle, the examples may be stories of spirit or character. From another angle, they're stories of belief—vignettes of commitment, trust, faith, hope, conviction and self-confidence, which are all siblings in the belief family.

Respiriting is, as we saw, a rebelieving; they're one and the same thing. Respiriting is reacquiring belief in one's self and one's company. The IBM manager we met on the beach (chapter 2) believed so much in the service ethic of his company that it caught in his throat and glistened in his eyes. That's an instance where belief becomes Spirit and Spirit is belief—both one and the same.

What was the Peters and Waterman (1982) book *In Search of Excellence* really about? Belief! Excellence was the topic, but believing in ourselves again was its real message. Housewives were reading it, as were school teachers, machine operators, plumbers—not just business-management types—everybody. Why? Right or wrong, the book was a shot of self-confidence for a nation and world with the shakes.

MOMENTS OF FAITH

Eventually our consideration of belief takes us far upstream to the headwaters where our cache of faith awaits the call. This is the place of wisdom, beyond mere knowledge; it is our highest knowing and yet beyond knowing. This is faith in oneself, not in anyone or anything external.

It's a faith that heads toward Spirit, that stems from Source deep within. It's not a visionless, unaware obedience to outside forces and pressures. It's Faith. "Blind faith," some say. In fact, there is no other kind; at this high level, if it weren't blind, it wouldn't be faith.

Some people find that concept hard to accept. They argue that faith is usually not blind. You have faith, they reason, because you have seen and understood at deep levels. You have faith in your spouse, for example, because he or she knows you and supports you. They assert that faith grows from seeing and knowing; in that sense, it is the opposite of blindness.

But that learned kind of faith comes from a way of thinking born of a legalistic/scientific mind-set that expects data and documentation.It may not be precisely scientific in the pure sense, but it is a common way of being in this world. Without thinking about it, people just come to expect proof. They become used to feeling comfortable only when living under the warm-blanket weight of evidence. Thus, they diminish their capacity; they begin to limit their store of trust, acceptance, and openness.

They become so locked into this way of thinking that it often takes something as extreme as a major illness to shake the current paradigm.

Only when thus shaken can they make the leap to faith. It's always a leap into the void because at those times there's simply no more "proof" to prop ourselves against. The point is that sooner or later we have to make the leap—we have to let go of understandable logic and make the big step beyond. And when that leap is made, the fall is usually straight up, toward Spirit.

There's quietness and serenity at these heights, closer to Spirit. This is the place of certainty, of moments of faith so high we merge with truth. This is where something at our core whispers "yes . . . yes" with full confidence. It brings the bounty of clarity, of seeing from higher self, the boon of being sure. This is when it all makes sense, when everything fits, when we know it's all happening as it is meant to, when we really understand that it is all okay.

This level of faith does *not* lead to stupid obedience to worldly level things or people. It's the exact opposite of that. This is the flowering of our own internal "evidence," the blooming of our own "proof," the creation of our own "authority."

Here repose moments of expanded capacity, instants of supreme quiet, brief periods of total acceptance, times of nonjudging, wondrous intervals when we know we're doing exactly, precisely what we're supposed to be doing. These are the gift times of supreme congruence, when thoughts and intuitions align like iron filings under a magnet, flashes of perfect order. Artists and scientists describe their highest work this way.

These wondrous moments of faith are rare, but they come to us all. It's our own inner knower knowing. It's the sounds of the universe in the seashell of ourselves. The world's clatter drowns it out most of the time, but when we are graced with hearing and can heed these sounds of certainty, we're fearless.

This is when Spirit visits and brings the boon of freedom from straining and railing, when we don't need to push against or defend against the world. That's the cosmic gift in this high belief: assuredness, faith, knowing, seeing, and connectedness. Those moments are a glimpse into the order of it, into Universal Truth, a truth born of belief. Spiritual truth.

CHAPTER 11

BENDING SPACE AND TIME:
ALREADY-THERENESS AND
INSTANTANEOUSNESS

The idea of quest is false.
—Sathya Sai Baba

We already are what we seek. Life is a matter of being what we are, not trying to become it. And that goes for our organizations as well. This is fundamentally a spiritual posture.

BENDING SPACE

The qualities we seek are already a part of us, not apart from us. We wouldn't yearn for them if they weren't already there. Our task is to *un*cover, not *dis*cover. We need to release it from inner space rather than seek it outside ourselves.

In *The Wizard of Oz*, Tin Man already had a heart, Scarecrow already had a brain, and Lion, his courage. Yet they yearned for those things. They had to endure many hard, scary adventures before they found those fabulous gifts. And where did they finally find them? Inside! Dorothy and Toto, too. They had to go through all that turmoil to get home, and it turns out they were dreaming, and that they were home all the time! There's a deep spiritual truth in that.

We can choose not to travel the yellow brick road. Rather than spend lifetimes trying to arrive "there," we can simply choose to already be there. It's a magical move from wanting-to-be, to being. It's a new angle on an ancient ploy: when we tell ourselves we're already there, we act that way;

and when we act that way, we become that way.

The term *space bending* fits, because that's what we do when we proclaim we're already "there." We warp from a not-there place to an already-there one. We move from trying to arrive somewhere to already residing in that place. By just declaring ourselves natives of the promised locale, we sidestep the less meaningful parts of the journey and become ready for the more important legs of the trip.

Just Be *One*

A score or more years ago when I was striving to become a management consultant, the magic of just *being* came home to me—literally. At the time my family was young, which added pressures on me to succeed. I perceived my life as revolving around learning the ropes, and I fretted some.

Louise kept saying, "Just be one." For months her words didn't register. It didn't sound reasonable; my logic blocked me. Just be one, indeed.

But the blockage wasn't total. The audaciousness of the idea appealed to me. I finally started to listen. Hmm, just be one! As that sank in, something happened to my practice. The focus on how to *become* one gradually dissolved, replaced by a clearer view of what I was currently doing.

A shift occurred. A different spirit began to take over. My internal dialogues began to match reality: "I'm now working as a consultant and doing quite well at it." Attention shifted from the work I was not yet doing to appreciating my present work.

As I grew to experience myself as a consultant, I realized the long-sought leap had already happened. Somewhere along the way I had bumped over from not-there-yet to there. I was already on the other side of the gap (see illustration below). That carried into my work. I saw things differently and naturally people looked at me differently.

My internal state rearranged itself to align with its "new" truth. My image, thoughts, and actions just rematerialized in the new place. Work became the delight I had hitherto hoped for. Naturally, quality improved.

Clients felt all this. As I came to believe in myself, so did they. As I came to be me, they more often asked me to be me with them. Suddenly I was off and running, not toward something new, but *as* something new.

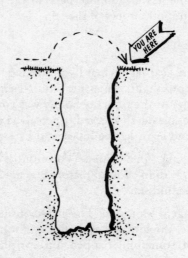

COATTAILING THE GRAIL

Ingrained in every living soul is the notion of search, the idea of striving to become. It's the metaphor of quest. It's the search for one's Spirit, the seeking of authenticity, the pursuit of the truth within. "Out there," intones a stage whisper inside, "are the priceless secrets of life; only the brave, the knightly may sally forth. The prize? No less than the rainbow's end, the meaning of life!" "Wow," we reply, and pack our duffel.

From this comes the prospector-explorer mind-set; thus, we have our own inner Ponce de Leons or Indiana Joneses, searching for fountains and lost arks. We spend life squinting, standing on tiptoes, eyes always drawn toward where the rainbow meets the earth. Questing fuels the furnaces of motivation and achievement. This is the stuff of heroes, isn't it?

Management planners ride the coattails of this energy, using it to achieve more mundane ends. The game goes like this: (1) detail out where we are now, (2) lay out where we want to be, (3) figure out how to get there,

(4) step out and go after it, and (5) check it out as you proceed. It's all neat, logical, and controllable.

The detailed analyses of our environment (step 1) comes, after all, from within ourselves—from what we think, see, feel, and hear. Then, the description of where we want to be (step 2), our goal, is articulated—also from within, drawn from our *own* vision and creativity. If we're smart, we make that "goal" seem so lip-smackin' good that we and others can't wait to taste it. (This is often where "visioning" comes in.)

The problem, however, occurs at step 2. Here's what happens: we go inside for the goal, get it firmly in hand, and then stretch to place it out in front of us. At that point we do a very weird thing. We set that juicy morsel out of reach. Like comic-strip donkeys, we take the carrot out of our own mouth and tie it on a stick suspended within sight and smell, but just out of bite range. Clack, clack (the sound of teeth biting air). And we use this contraption to entice us onward.

I've used the approach myself thousands of times. I've taught it for over a generation. I'm not tossing it away; I still believe in having goals and going after them. That's the way we've done things, and it has done wonders for us.

But we're on the other side now, in a new era, with different rules. One of the rules is, "You're already there!" Doing it the usual way, with the starting assumption that we're not there, is a negative proclamation to our inner being. "You're not" is the message. On the other hand, an already-thereness attitude invites the space-bending mentioned above. Assuming that we already have "it" skips us to a new place. No more clack, clack. Energy previously spent striving returns—and things seem to work better.

THE SPIRIT OF ALREADY-THERENESS

The familiar idea of searching-to-grow, exciting though it may be, is a gap maker. The long-cherished notion of *becoming* can soothe, but it can also serve to distance us from ourselves rather than bring us nearer. The spirit of already-thereness, on the other hand, is a gap closer. *Being* has more power in it than *becoming*.

Imagine just proclaiming already-thereness. No questions asked. No permission sought. Simply take residence. It's audacious, but declaring it is what creates it. That's the leap!

The good leader-manager does it more than we realize. Take Iacocca's heralded rescue of Chrysler. Regardless of later problems, at the time it was a remarkable, heroic rescue. Everybody had counted them out. "Forget it," the experts said. To them, the company was already just another Studebaker, a prairie wagon, a nostalgic memory. The planners, with good intentions, schemed rescue after rescue, all of which were, in effect, proclamations of not-thereness.

But Lee kept saying, "We are healthy. We are okay. Our cars are already good. Our labor contracts will be good." Most people thought he was nuts to be declaring health at such an obviously ill time. But his strong proclamations served to bring power. Pronouncing health, happiness, and strength beckons those states from within. Call it affirmation, positive thinking, believing, faith, hypnotism, autosuggestion, or programming; whatever it's called, it works.

It's simply not powerful to impute weakness to oneself. Our fore—fathers didn't ask people to sign a "petition" of independence, they declared it! The late author-lecturer Buckminster Fuller, encouraging people to find their own power, says he never signed petitions. "Petitions signal a lack of power," he hrrumph'd.

> A retail pharmacy company wanted to make a quantum leap in customer relations. Although very successful (doing $500 million a year and growing), top management wasn't happy with the way customers were treated.
>
> Sophisticated, they talked of the need to "transform their culture." After eighteen months of hard work—surveys, focus groups, comparison studies, customer profiles, lots of charts and graphs—they came up with a great plan for doing it.
>
> They pictured what "there" (excellent customer relations) would look like. They wrote great descriptions of what excellent staff-customer encounters would feel like. They developed nice definitions of politeness, sales, and service. And they mapped out a detailed path to get there. Included along the way were better systems for employee selection and training, plus monitoring schemes to make sure that they carried out all these activities. They estimated it to be a five-year trip.
>
> Note what they did: they reached into their own experience, their own intellect, their own intimate knowledge of their own organization's performance, and from within themselves came out with a beautiful definition of what they thought

was a goal. But it wasn't really a goal. They thought it was, but it was a description of what already existed in many parts of the organization, and in their own hearts.

They didn't need a big program to teach and monitor people's behavior. People already knew what "excellent customer relations" meant. But, being conscientious manager-planners, they labeled their work "goal," which snatched it up and put it out of reach. Instant chasm.

We consultants arrived on the scene at that point. The managers all talked agreement with the plan. They wanted it to be great, but their shuffling gave it away. Their words: "I like it"; their body language (shoulders slumped, frowns, tongues lolling): "I hate it."

We respected the people who crafted the plan and wanted to believe it ourselves, but we couldn't get past the dank cloud of dejection hovering over the place. Finally, I looked at the CEO and members of the planning task force and swallowed, "You must not spend five years on this." Heads lifted, people looked around as if shaken awake. The nonverbal sigh of relief emboldened me. "A few revisions of your plan, and you can do it in, say, five months." They got busy immediately on the revisions.

The spirit of already-thereness entered the plan. The first phase originally called for a unit-by-unit assessment of current performance against the goal. Logical, but it would've widened the gulch.

The revised plan had them identify units that were good examples of excellent customer relations. Where the early plan required managers to reveal performance problems, the new one required them to ferret out top-performing units.

Other revisions reflected the same thread (which was the truth): we're already okay, we're already doing it right! The new program was designed to pass and reinforce this message to all fifteen hundred employees.

And did they catch it! Over the next twelve months the entire organization systematically held up its islands of merit, its bastions of excellent customer relations. "These are our exemplars!" they trumpeted. This is how the word spread of the new expectations.

The basic message wasn't new—everybody knows customer relations are important. It was the spirit that was new. "*This is us*," it proclaimed; "this is how we do it." It didn't say, "This is how we hope to do it someday." Expectations were crystal clear. Local units moved to make sure their performance was in line. It was all so painless. Already-thereness usually is.

BENDING TIME

> *Instantaneousness leading to transformation, rather than process leading to change.*
> —Zen master

> *There are no steps . . . . There is nothing gradual about it. It happens suddenly and is irreversible. You rotate into a new dimension.*
> —Nisargadatta

Instantaneousness is ancient wisdom flying in the face of current knowledge. It's the daring idea that massive change can, and often does, happen in the blink of an eye. "Whoa!" shout many of my old friends. "That can't be! Everybody knows change takes a long time!" One man, a friend of a friend, sprang at me. I was at a local university talking about Instantaneousness. "Look," he quivered, thin-lipped, "I'm a therapist and I know that changing requires a very, very long time!"

He left Los Angeles before we had an opportunity to finish our talk. Too bad. If I were to beam him back here now, I would say, "Well, it's a matter of what you believe. If you believe change takes a very long time, it will. My belief is that there are situations where change can and does occur in what is for the person or organization a mere finger snap. That fast— click!—and a new entity is popped into being. And these situations are far more prevalent than we allow. Given the right conditions, change can flash over a human system, whether individual, organization, society, or world."

Lightening Change

From where did this hair-trigger idea come? Those hundreds of hours of discussion in the consultants' symposium back in Los Angeles (preface) helped fetch the idea from wherever it had hidden. We wanted to better understand change, remember, and were searching for the very soul of human-systems transformation. That required journeying into our own souls and undergoing deep change ourselves. Transformation demands confrontation of ingrained beliefs. Uncomfortable? Sort of, but exhilarating too.

After months of soul-searching, we came face-to-face with our ingrained belief that change takes a long time. Who graffitied the walls of our minds with that idea? Closer examination revealed cracks in those walls. We had been going along with the old shibboleth that personal and organizational change require eons. But maybe change doesn't have to take that long! Might it occur faster? Could it happen in an eye-blink? After all, doesn't the notion of transformation have within it "flashes" of insight and "moments" of awakening? Isn't sudden, intuitive knowing an integral part of it?

The brash idea of split-second change propelled us beyond the dogma barrier into a buoyant state. The problems and dilemmas of change became lighter in both senses of the word: less heavy and less dark. Lightening change, indeed. Several professionals in the change business didn't like the idea much; it's a little upsetting, having your old graffiti scrubbed.

A few years ago, friend Lynne asked if I would work on a consulting project at a hospice. I was busy and begged off. She pleaded that I at least go there for one day to help get the project started. "Okay, one day," I said.

The hospice turns out to be a terminal cancer unit for patients within a few weeks of death. The staff consists of people who drift toward this special field. They're special people who work at the biggest transformation in people's lives. Talk about growth change! They're always toiling at the border where life force crosses over to wherever it goes.

Their job is to dignify the passage. Helping people die well may sound gloomy, but it's not. The work consists primarily of relieving pain: the physical pain suffered by patients and the pain of loneliness at this utterly alone time for patients and families. The staff is there for them—giving, caring, holding hands, bolstering spirits, guiding. The work is chock full of purpose and meaning seldom felt by most working people.

The start-up day is interesting. We get a tour of the facility. It has prettier walls than a hospital, feels a bit quieter and more human, but it's essentially the same. Then we visit the "saying good-bye room." It's furnished as a home bedroom: queen bed, dresser, lamps, and such. When patients die, the bodies are put on the bed in this room where family and friends can sit with them, say prayers, good-byes, or just be alone together.

As I step over the threshold into the softly lit room, some-thing flutters over me. I'm neither a spiritualist nor a "sensi-tive," but I can feel something different there—a stirring, a faint inner quickening comes. No fear in it; it's a "beyond" feeling. An inner whisper comes, "Much to learn here." I accept the assignment.

The management problems they called us for are fairly standard except, we find out, for one situation which they term the morale problem. One group of nurses is down in the dumps and is dragging the whole organization with them.

A feature of this hospice is that the care of the patients occurs both in their homes and in the hospice itself. The aim is to keep people in familiar surroundings as much as possible during this time. As the illness ebbs and flows, the patients are admitted to the unit, then sent home, readmitted, sent home again, and so on, until the end.

Two sets of nurses tend the patients: an inpatient team and a home care team. The sets are like bookends: same age range, training, life values, interests. They do essentially the same work, with the same population of patients and families. But the inpatient group is airy, the outpatient group dank. They're the ones in the dumps, and it is affecting (infecting) the whole place.

The second day, I talk with small groups of inpatient nurses. It's an impressive day. These are truly loving, dedicated people—giving service and helping patients and their families bring a richness to both their work and home lives. At the end of the day they ask me to stay for the family potluck dinner. Once a week the patients' relatives bring in food from home and everyone gets together in the lounge— patients, nurses, administrators, and support staff. A variety of dishes show up on these nights, including ethnic dishes and special favorites prepared with loving care.

It's more than food. Each dish carries a loving, human connection. The atmosphere is easygoing and warm. People have pretty much dropped their masks and are content to just be with one another and enjoy that. Good conversation, good food, good people, good company.

But all those "goods" are spoiled goods the next day. The home care nurses rudely yank me into their version of reality! The calm and quiet of yesterday turns into clanging. Serenity is replaced by "Ain't it awful!" They're completely negative. Their whole lives are tainted by their badmouthing and bad thinking. Yesterday's heaven is today's hell—both spaces created by the people themselves.

They had heard I was coming and are ready to spring. Every fifth word is *burnout*. The overused metaphor has become the reality of their lives. Nothing remains now but their own charred bones.

Every day is a drag for them. To hear them tell it, they drag from bed and drag themselves into worn-out cars. Then they stress out on freeways, only to suffer through attempts to provide care to "impossible" patients and "uncooperative" families in inhospitable homes. They've languaged them- selves into a snit. They're more practiced at nursing a grudge than at nursing.

No one is spared. The administrator is insensitive and she doesn't listen, the parent company is insensitive and doesn't care, the staff psychologist may be sensitive but doesn't seem to do anything. They're feeling forlorn, forsaken, forgotten. I hear the word *insensitive* until I'm, well, numb.

I try to listen and try to empathize with their choler, but the echoes of yesterday are still in me. The place can't be that bad, I think. I try not to drift from their tirade lest I, too, am labeled insensitive. The extra effort tightens me up. My voice starts to pinch. I have to strain to stay alert. My energy tiptoes away. Sooner or later I'll have to come clean with them, and what then? Will they do me in like they're doing everyone else? I fantasize the group screaming, "You lout, you're not listening; you're like all the others!"

Midafternoon. We've just reconvened after a break. I'm sitting, facing the dour dozen. It's showdown time. I make eye contact with a few and that bolsters, but I'm still afraid my feedback will trigger the attack. They have said nothing all day that would lead me to believe that they want to work out the problem, but I've got to believe they do.

Finally, I suck in a breath and say what I am feeling, seeing, and hearing. They sit mum. In essence, I tell them that somewhere along the line they've crossed over into total negativity, that they're all creating a hell for themselves. I say, "You start every day believing it's going to be bad, and thus it is. You're living a self-fulfilling prophecy. Every time there's a choice of going sweet or sour, you pick the stinky path. You program yourselves negatively in the morning, and through-out the day you reprogram often to stay on that path. You're playing an awful game of 'ain't-it-awful,' so no wonder it feels so awful. And you can't seem to break that pattern . . . and I'm troubled by that."

Finished talking, I sit back, breathing a little heavily. That's a long speech for me. They sit blankly. Are they listening? They seemed attentive—or is it suppressed anger? The silence continues, the air is uneasy. I figure it's either attack time or work time.

One of the more outspoken women's body language indicates she's getting ready to talk. She returns my look, takes a breath, and says, "Y'know . . . my husband is a cop. He's always so negative. Everything is bad, bad, bad, from the minute he walks in the door." The others are visibly relieved the silence is broken.

She continues, "The TV we watch is bad. The movies we go

to are bad. The other night we were driving down the street and he sees two normal, long-haired kids, and he says they're probably junkies or something. You can't go anywhere with him . . ." She shakes her head sadly and looks down at her hands.

Then the woman next to her leans toward me and asks seriously, "How can we stop doing this?" The others chorus, "Yes! How can we?" With that—*Fwoosh!*—the pall lifts, the room brightens. Everything lightens—facial expressions, postures, intensity, the energy level, people's fatigue level— everything! It's as if the magnetic field in the room suddenly about-faces to positive! It dawns: they don't want to be that way, they're more sick of it than anyone.

We all relax and spend the rest of the session conferring about various methods for achieving and retaining positive states of mind. The conversation may be informative, but it's really just mop-up. The flip into higher spirit has already occurred, and it's profound.

A whole new set of rules was adopted that instant. "Our life *will* be better from now on" sums it up. No one bothered to list the new rules, but everyone immediately felt them. Sure, the system was ripe for such a change; and yes, the moment of transformation had more leading up to it than I'm de- scribing; and of course, considerable follow-up work had to be done. But that's prologue and epilogue. The point is the flash of change.

Within hours all the other employees in the hospice felt the shift in this group's mood. The whole place lit up. You could feel the change of humor and could almost hear the collective sigh of relief. They didn't have to wallow for years through surveys, training sessions, and problem-solving meetings. All they did is pivot toward light.

Shazam!

I've observed the same flash of instantaneous change in organizations much larger and more conventional than the hospice. As with the hospice, all they needed was a spark. That "moment" of ignition in a larger system may be spread over days or weeks, but for them it's relatively a moment.

Those flashes are startling and dramatic. They bring goose bumps; they're tears-in-the-eyes times, when the system bursts into a whole new mode of being—moments of epiphany, of death and resurrection, of new-sprung energy, heart, and spirit.

Here's a quick story of one of those times.

A large government fire-fighting organization struggles with grave safety problems. For twenty years the wrestling match has continued, and they're losing. An average of six or seven employees are killed every year in fire-suppression accidents!

Being a government bureaucracy, they're constantly "fixed" from above. Headquarters is frantic to win this match. Blizzards of directives, policies, and regulations blow in from the Washington office. Every conceivable safety training course is stuffed into them, and new ones are invented. Two university-based research projects try to get a handle on the problem, but the reports yellow on the shelf. Nothing works! The ingrained behavior of employees continues as it was— and every year more people die. The organization keeps getting slammed to the mat.

Finally, they launch a massive employee involvement pro-gram. Over an eleven-month period, a trained team system-atically involves all sixty-two hundred fire fighters, managers, and even outside contractors in a no-nonsense program to diagnose and resolve their own safety issues.

The result: a miracle! The wrestling match is suddenly over; it's a clean pin! The first year, no deaths. Second year, no deaths. Third year, the same. And it continues. Safety has apparently become a strong new habit.

In the twelve years following the program there is only one accidental death. Just one! Headquarters is ecstatic. The CEO gets a special award, and everyone connected with the project is promoted. It's like a Hollywood movie: bring up the music, fade to the sun setting over the now-peaceful mountains . . .

We can hooray the happy ending, but that's not the point. This is a story of instantaneousness. The flash of transformation comes three months into the program. The organization's fifty top managers—its power structure—are attending a three-day feedback session. It is the first time they are hearing the reports of the inquiry teams.

J. J., a respected executive fire fighter, is obviously in pain. He sits glumly as the unvarnished comments of rank-and-file fire fighters are recounted. He winces at some of the quotes: "Can't buy badly needed safety equipment due to red tape." "Only gung ho [unsafe] supervisors get promoted." "You can't blow the whistle on poor safety around here." The day is full of those. When it ends, people wander off in shock.

First thing the next morning, without waiting for the CEO to open the meeting, J. J. clears his throat and nervously starts to talk. His face is ashen. "I don't want to believe that feedback," he says, his voice shaking. "I talked to my wife about it for a long time last night—and I didn't sleep very well." He pauses, close to tears, staring into the distance, perhaps recalling the many years and the many accidents.

The room hushes. J. J. starts to apologize, but the CEO asks him to continue and others signal agreement. Steadied, he begins again, "But, as much as it hurts, I believe it . . . we all must believe it . . . and we have to do something about it."

Fwoosh! That's the instant. J. J.'s truth speaks for all. His pain and remorse for lost comrades, his frustrations at having allowed the situation to continue for so long, and his deep sorrow touch the group's heart and release Spirit. Energy surges through the group; it's the vitality that comes with integrity. The atmosphere in the room crackles as archaic ways die. These old-pro managers become caught up in the excitement and momentum of instantaneous transformation.

I'm so excited I can't sit. I walk over to the side wall and stand with Brian, the safety staffperson whose strategic goading got the program started. Gordon, a headquarters executive who is there as an observer, is standing with us. His eyes dart nervously from the unfolding scene to me and back. It seems a little out of control to him. He can feel the crackle and sizzle but doesn't yet grasp the sheer magnitude of the transformation taking place. I do. "Shazam!" I mutter to myself.

The managers spend the remaining two days looking one another in the eye and hammering out the tough agreements and action plans that eventually bring about that miraculous Hollywood ending. Lots of follow-up will be needed afterward, but Instantaneousness has struck.

CHAPTER 12

UNTETHERING FROM WORLDLY LIFE: TRUE FREEDOM

Possessions exhaust us.
— B. Chatwin

*To attain knowledge, add things
every day. To attain wisdom,
remove things every day.*
— Lao-tzu

*Cultivate detachment and God
will attach to you.*
— Sathya Sai Baba

We all become snared by worldly things—goods, possessions, relation-ships, personal comfort—that we think are important but really aren't. It's a pattern of dependence on the wrong things. It's an addiction. We're not in control, the habit is. Thus tied up, we're held back from our real mission, which is to move toward spirit and achieve a fuller experience of life.

After a while these tethers hurt. Like some giant Velcro fastener, they hold us firmly against worldly life, smothering our freedom. The obvious remedy is to unhook and go in the other direction, to move toward less possessions and attachments. But decreasing the girth size of our material life is a maverick idea in Western cultures. It's outlandish and unheard of!

We just keep on fattening our lives with *things*. "More, only more" is the rule.

But detachment and freedom are synonymous. To detach from things is to become uncaught by them. Rather than running faster to collect more (whether it's possessions, power, affection, or prestige), it is better to detach and make space for spirit. Our life is far more meaningful than what we accumulate during it.

Detachment means letting go of attitudes and beliefs that hold us back, as well as letting go of belongings. It requires lopping off old emotional traumas that consume energy and interfere with moving ahead. It even means becoming less entangled with family—not abandoning them but loving them with fewer strings.

Untethering from all this is a mental leave-taking, not necessarily a physical one. It's not a giving up of worldly things; it's a releasing from the desire for and dependence on those things. Thus, you don't relinquish enjoyment of life; rather, you set yourself free from the inevitable disappointments and disquiet that come from being addicted to these trappings, these snares of life.

As I write this chapter in India, a succession of images comes. First, I see a burro, common in the crowded village streets. It's small, mostly brown, almost woolly despite the searing heat. Its markings include a black cross that sits athwart its back and shoulders—a cross so perfect the Christians assumed these were the beasts that carried Christ.

The villagers often tie the burro's front feet together to keep it from wandering too far. I see them hobbling, heads down, and hear the sounds of their scuffling, each step a crippled skip that requires a little jump with both feet to bump forward. The animals take it in stride, so to speak, apparently resigned to this man-made lameness and the resultant inability to go beyond certain boundaries.

Then, I see the mighty elephant with its enormous brain and great learning abilities. Powerful beasts. When first brought into captivity, their feet are chained to several stakes driven deeply into firm ground. They must be thus anchored or they would range free again.

But they too learn. The pressure against their ankles teaches them to stay in place. Soon the stout anchoring stake at the end of the chain can be replaced by a peewee peg pushed easily into soft earth. The merest tug and it would yank free, but the huge beast sticks around. The scant pressure against its ankle triggers a stay-in-your-place program driven deep into its brain.

An additional clincher has to do with Jumbo's new human friends: a dependence on the handler develops. At first, it's for food and water; after a while, it's just habit. It's another mental program, and the combined programs are stronger than the mighty muscles. So the mammoth beast stays, and stays—freedom remembered perhaps, but not vividly enough to yank out the peg.

BARRIERS IN THE PATH

Next, a reverie vision of Ahbleza comes to me from Ruth Beebe Hill's (1983) magnum opus novel, *Hanta Yo.*

> Ahbleza is a Sioux warrior, son of a chief and perhaps soon to be chief himself. He is contemplating marriage to Hayatawin, the proud-walking woman. Life's tethers are compounding for him. Ahbleza is happy, but there's something lacking.
>
> In his sleep he hears Wanagi, the medicine man, his friend, who is like a father to him, calling. He arises, loads a pipe, and goes to Wanagi's lodge. The medicine man refuses the pipe, lighting his own instead. They sit, not speaking.
>
> Ahbleza finally talks of his many worldly concerns: worries about the coming of winter, about how many horses to pay for the bride, about others' expectations of a future chief. He speaks of his father's influence over him, about going on one more hunt before settling down alongside a woman, and about how he usually handles barriers by going around them instead of removing them.
>
> Wanagi sits, not answering. His face reflects the dancing light from the fire. After a second pipeful, he speaks one phrase, *"Wahpani iciya wo"* (Throw out everything). The phrase could be interpreted many ways, but Ahbleza, ever the warrior, decides to take it as a command. Start again. Regard yourself as a newborn.

Renew yourself completely. He begins immediately.

"Let the people see a man who tests himself," he grits, "one who throws off everything he accumulates—including any thoughts other persons have given him that were originally not his own." He gives away all his robes and the hides used for lodge covering. He gives away his horses, making himself foot-going; then he gives away his final pair of moccasins. He gives away his lances, bows, knives, every weapon he owns except his hands. He gives until nothing exists for him but his person. And then he discards from his mind whoever or whatever outside of himself influences him.

Finally, wearing only a loincloth, he leads his one remaining horse, his favorite, and ties it at the last lodge in the long line of lodges—a gift for the crippled boy whose family has nothing. "Until he walks, this horse will carry your son gently," he tells the mother.

Then Ahbleza turns and walks to the other side of the knoll. He unties the string at his waist, his loin cover falls to the ground. "I will live with my bareness, out of view, until I know I am truly loyal to myself. Only then will I dare to walk as a chief." He walks away onto the plains, alone.

The story of the writing of *Hanta Yo* is itself an engaging example of detachment and personal power. For almost a generation author Ruth Hill worked to construct her story of the Plains Indians as they were before white influence. But she still wasn't satisfied with it; the book lacked something. Then, in the seventeenth year of writing, she met Chunska Yuha. He was in his seventies, the last remaining of eight boys who were sheltered from white man's influence during their childhood and taught the archaic language and customs of their people.

Chunska Yuha called Hill's journey until then one of blindness because she was trying to construct a bridge to an ancient spiritual people through the language and nonspiritual interpretations of white men. She had to discard almost every concept relative to Indians ever formed. ("Become ruthless, Ruth.") The core notions contained in all those years of work had to be tossed out.

Ruth and Chunska Yuha translated the two-thousand-page second draft of the book into the old Lakota tongue and then back into English.

This would, she hoped, infuse it with heart and truth. As they worked, the book took on a new substance—a verve, an energy began to flow through each sentence. Now within the pages flowed *taku skan-skan* (something-in-movement, spiritual vitality).

This woman could not stop short of her truth. Only by untethering from her life's work could the work become whole and complete. I'm reminded of Robert Penn Warren's comment to the effect that only when careerism dies does life spurt.

Detaching

Still thinking about Ahbleza's detaching (he went on, by the way, to become a great chief), and reflecting on Ruth Hill's ready releasing from her great, almost lifelong project, I'm reminded of my talk with Liz.

Liz was the director of a large company. One of the turning points in her life had come a couple of years before when her house burned down. All the family's belongings went poof, up in smoke. I cringe, "Must have been tough." "Not really," she dismisses it, "it was quite freeing. No one was hurt, there wasn't anything of real value. Oh, I may miss the piano a little, but we learned a lot. All those material things are unimportant."

Then, I think of how emotional bonds to family hold us long after physical bonds are torn away. I'm reminded that even family, as important as it is, has to be transcended. I recall Robin and Ortrud saying good-bye to their shining six-year-old as he went off to Sai Baba's boarding school three blocks distant. Such a little guy, and such big tears in his eyes as he pulled away—and even bigger ones behind his father's eyes. So young, and missed so much at first.

Cutting ties to family isn't abandonment. The ties to be cut are internal. It's not a question of shirking responsibility. People don't necessarily leave physically. It's a matter of loving more purely. It's a matter of giving up dependency on others and setting it up so they can do the same.

I recall our neighbor Yvonne's stranglehold on husband Jim and the kids. In the name of wife and mother she clutches too tightly. This goes on for years; the dependency suffocates them and is equally stifling to her. When Jim finally breaks the clench and walks out for good, she's devastated and needs to be hospitalized.

Later, as the self-placed yokes are gradually unhooked, her health comes back. First, she lets go of Jim—inside. It's a releasing from her own dependence on him. Then, she loosens the ties to her son in college, leaves her job, sells the house, and bids good-bye to the neighborhood and friends.

As each bond is snipped, you can see her begin to stand and walk straighter, her voice becomes surer, eyes clearer. Like a stop-action movie of an opening flower, flick-flick-flick, frame by frame, she goes from doleful grays to vibrant hues. Life is not easy for her during these healing months, but it's better. *Taku skan-skan* begins to flow; she becomes something-in-movement herself.

There is a growing acceptance in the West of the principle of detachment. Phyllis Krystal (1984), a psychotherapist working in detachment therapy, is totally dedicated to cutting the ties that bind. The primary emphasis in her work is to help people release from the burdens of emotional attachments and past traumas.

She does it in an interesting way. She and the client first visualize themselves connected together as partners. Then, still connected, they visualize themselves connected upward to a combined higher consciousness. At this level, their higher selves are really one. They use this joint connection with higher consciousness (call it Spirit) to rise beyond regular psychology, and to invoke the wisdom and guidance of higher consciousness. They release from worldly ties by retying to Spirit.

Krystal has also written about a structured approach to detachment called Ceiling on Desires (program concept developed in India by Sathya Sai Baba). This program tackles four categories of attachment in people's lives: money, food, time, and energy. By meditating on a set of questions (where, in my life, am I wasting money? wasting food? and so forth), people gain insights from their higher self about ways to cut down dependence in each of the categories.

The idea of detachment is also at work in Neuro-Linguistic Programming (Grinder and Bandler 1981). They call it dissociation. It consists of such techniques as imagining oneself stepping clear of bonds and physically moving away from problems. In this way, people solve knotty personal issues from a distance, unsnarled in them. Being free of the problems facilitates resolution of them, which is often the only way they can be handled.

The field of psychosynthesis also emphasizes releasing. It reaches beyond the physical/mental being to what practitioners call the transpersonal—the beyond-body, higher self. Transpersonal psychologists borrow from ancient jnana yoga (the yoga of wisdom) and repeat: I have a body, but I am not my body; I have emotions, but I am not my emotions; I have an intellect, but I am not my intellect; I have a mind, but I am not my mind.

What remains? Pure consciousness, an awareness of one's true essence and sense of being—the real you (Spirit, again).

All of these approaches help us stay in the game and be more effective in it—by getting away from it. Moving into the higher-self realm makes it easier to handle worldly problems. Effective leaders instinctively know the value of doing this; hence, the calls for "altitude" and "vision" nowadays.

Resizing Life

> Not long ago, Paul Terhorst, a CPA, the youngest full partner in a big-eight accounting firm, is obviously on the fast track to the big time; nonetheless, he quits. He looks at his high-achiever life and finds it hollow. Over a two-year period he and his wife do some responsible financial figuring and a lot of soul-searching about what's really important in their life. They decide to transform their life pattern. He (Terhorst 1988) has written a book about it.

> This young, upwardly mobile professional, like some throw-back to the 1960s, decides to hang up his cleats to live a life that offers him more meaning than corporate life does. The first yuppie-hippie. Certainly not rich, but knowing how to manage money, they sell most of their possessions and use the proceeds to live at a less material level. Now they spend more time traveling, reading, writing, and studying. To them, it's a more natural way of living.

> Paul is not advocating this for everybody, but the lessons he (they) learned while attempting to simplify things are instructive. The hardest part, he says, is going against the norms and expectations of friends and family. A strong norm in this society is that you must work, that you must progress in a career, and that you ought to do it until retirement age. It's a matter of whether or not to postpone personal emancipation until later in life. It's even harder going against your own conditioning, trying to erase the unwritten inner rules about work, accomplishment, possessions, and such.

> Those unwritten messages from society are case-hardened steel tethers. Breaking free of them is the hardest thing Paul

has ever done. It takes him two years to make the parting, and then another two years afterward to work it through and become comfortable with it.

Here's another story, closer to home this time.

A few years ago Louise and I are at the point in our lives where the issue of detachment is magnified. Little by little, our material world has become immaterial; matter doesn't seem to matter as much. Yet we feel hooked by it. Preferring to grow, rather than just continue to get heavier, we consider reducing our worldly life to make room for the spiritual.

One day Louise walks in and says, "It just came to me, we must get ready to go now." I don't know what she means, but she has the same throw-out-everything look I imagine Wanagi had when he talked to Ahbleza. I watch with wry interest as she starts to work on her office.

The two plump Rolodexes go first. They're her power; they're the essence of the networking from her events-promotion business. If stacked, the address cards on the two rolls would be three feet high. She decides to cull out the cards that she feels won't be relevant; she sits for three days, pulling and tearing each card. One by one, worldly contact by worldly contact, the cards are ripped in half. Hundreds of tiny ceremonial triumphs: rip-rip-save-rip. The only ones that escape are those she really wants. When done, less than an inch of the stack remains.

Next, her files go up the chimney in smoke—literally. We sit in front of the fireplace for another three days as she stokes the flames with records of past projects. Alive only a moment ago, the segments of her professional past dance before us in the flames, one last incandescence before becoming ash.

One afternoon Louise comes in and challenges, "Do you wanna sell your Porsche?" My retort, "Wanna cut off your private phone line?" We gulp in unison, "Yes." The next day both are gone.

Our scrutiny then turns to our living accommodations, assessing what we actually need versus what we have. Living

so modestly in India and Mexico affords us the good perspective that what we have here far exceeds needs or wants.
"When in doubt, toss it out" becomes the rule. Away goes
most of the furniture.

The only way to deal with the storage stuff—the garage-attic
monster, we call it—is to hack away at it. Each box we dig
through contains nostalgic and dusty memories, and they're all
tethers. Each memory requires a brutal toss-or-keep decision.

We notice that the more we toss, the lighter we feel! Each
landfill-sized load out the door removes the dross of decades.
As each box of possessions is given to Goodwill, life feels
more in balance, less cluttered. Like Yvonne and Liz and
Paul, like Ahbleza and Ruth Hill, gradually our life becomes,
well, more, as our ties to it are fewer.

Finally, the grand uprooting. We rent out our too-big house
and move into a smaller place.

It takes two full years to gradually resize our life, paring it
down to about 25 percent of what it was. With that divesting
have come a simplicity and balance in our lives that are
invaluable to us. And yes, it is the hardest thing we've ever
done. Would we do it again? Well, the memories of how
difficult it was have faded and our life is indeed lighter and
simpler. The thought of becoming thing-bound and heavy-
lived again makes us shudder.

EMANCIPATING SPIRIT

Friend Ben was one of the wry watchers of our downsizing. He's still
working at age sixty-five and doesn't even think of retiring. He can't
comprehend life unhandcuffed to work—it's illogical to him, it simply
doesn't register. He's scared to death of retirement.

Aha! So that's it. Death is the issue! Death comes when the final box
is thrown out of the dusty attic, when the ultimate fastener unfastens. Run
out the logic : if each tether links us to life, then as each one is released, it
brings the Reaper a bit closer. Totally unhook and what happens? You
become ash along with your possessions. "No thanks, I prefer entangle-
ments" is the understandable reaction.

But we really shouldn't worry about that. Ben's line of reasoning can't be extended out indefinitely. Becoming free of everything in life would be impossible. We're here to live this life—richly—and we must do that *in* the world. And that means we must deal with worldly matters.

We don't shrivel up as we unload, we emancipate. Each knot released does not bring us closer to death, it brings us nearer life! It's a question of whether we want to live Velcroed to worldly stuff or be free of it. It's not a matter of one or the other, though; it's balance again. Too much worldly, and Spirit is unable to soar. Better we send out one shining thread tied securely to Spirit than remain ensnared with the worldly.

Another aha! So it's Spirit again. All material things, especially when overdepended on, keep us from Spirit. The upper circle shrinks as the lower circle fattens (see illustration below). In the overstuffed lower circle are the ropes of attachment. Desires for security and comfort are in that circle; it's also the repository of old traumas to which we're still hooked.

They're all fetters, all hobbles. They're tin lids on our jar of life. They're our mental and mettle ceilings, and they're all freedom-robbing hooks. Blam! we're pressed flat against that world and held so tightly we can't breathe. James Thurber's plaintive comment comes to mind: that he would run off to some South Seas island but his orthodontist would get angry.

To detach from all these things is to become uncaught by worldly life; it's a mental leave-taking, not a physical one. It's not enjoyment that is being given up, remember, it's desire, need, sorrow, and lack of peace. Without those, we can live an even more peaceful, more fulfilled life. As the lower self recedes, higher Self clarifies. That again is the purpose of life after all: to come to a realization of Self and achieve this peace. That's why untethering is so potent and so important!

> Sai Baba comes out on the veranda and talks with several people about living life in tune with Spirit. Someone says, "But the spiritual life is such hard work." Baba feigns surprise. "What? Hard work?" he says, a mock frown on his face. He extends a clenched fist, palm upward, gripping a handkerchief, saying, "Holding on is hard work." Then he flips it over and lets it drop. "Letting go is easy," he says and walks away.

PART IV

RECHARACTERING

STRENGTHENING PERSONAL AND ORGANIZATIONAL INTEGRITY

This section is about the awesome idea of living by one's inner truth. It asserts that character is what makes the whole recipe of life work, determining whether we gag on life or savor it. The concept of dharma from the East is affixed to integrity, drawing to it the energies of rightness, spirit, and fearlessness—creating a superintegrity. A prescription for recharactering is included here that applies to individuals and organizations.

CHAPTER 13

LIVING BY YOUR INNER TRUTH

*Some say knowledge is power,
but that is not true. Character
is power.*

—Sathya Sai Baba

Character is the distinguishing feature, the essence, the basic ingredient in the new management paradigm. It can give organizational life a heartiness and a uniqueness that are too often compromised nowadays. People hunger for character.

The term *character* refers to a cluster of interlaced ideas and social virtues that includes morality, ethics, honesty, and human values. In the management workplace, character consists of integrity and dharma.

WANTING CHARACTER

We need to look long and hard at what *character* means and why it is so urgent in today's hard-driving world. We need to examine how to infuse it into our daily lives and the lives of our organizations.

All that? And more. More! We need help on this. Let's reconvene the Handy Panel of executives who were so straightforward earlier and see what they have to say. I again ask them to give me the straight scoop—this time on character in the workplace. They're a bit subdued, but true to form, they leap right into it without worrying about niceties:

"Ethics and morality? Honesty? You're kidding! Good topics for church or campus, maybe, but not talked about in the halls and conference rooms around our companies. Sure, we feel some responsibility for this, but we've got work to do, y'know."

"It was guile, nimbleness, and keeping our noses clean that helped us get here. Maybe they aren't the only factors, but they helped. Didn't we tell you it's a competitive world out there? You maneuver for position or you're in the back of the pack, Jack."

"*Honesty, truthfulness, fairness, right and wrong*—they're half-empty words. Just more "shoulds" to make people feel inadequate. How about these words: *compete, deceit, exploit, expediency, self-interest,* and *bottom-line-or-else*?"

"When push comes to shove, forget that nice stuff and produce, baby, or else! We're not even saying that's bad, but that's the way it really is. Values statements are sort of a deception. They look pretty, and feel solid in good times, but under pressure the veneer peels."

"Greed is the name of the song nowadays! Greedy for money, power, status, just about anything. Will it never end? The more money they—well, we—make, the more we grab. Everybody's doing it, so if you don't, it seems dumb."

"We're not saying everybody's a big crook, but they're all little ones. People think nothing of accepting small 'gifts' and taking home little things. It's so commonplace people think it's natural. Everybody's doing it, so why not me?"

"It's the pattern: take, take, take. After a while taking becomes second nature. Giving? You don't even think about it. Just take, take. You just never give it a thought."

"You have to play it that way—always on the make, exploiting, using the system and the people in it, getting the most out of it. Ha! Everybody milks the organization for more, more. Then they talk about how alienated they feel from it."

"It's not the occasional big corruption that gets to you, it's the little ones that debase us all and eat away at us: playing favorites, politicking, withholding information, cozying up for favors, manipulating, jockeying for position. None of it is against the law, but it feels dirty. And worse, you get good at it after a while."

"Fact is, y'gotta make a living; and to do that, you've got to be in an organization; and to be in one without self-destructing, you have to compromise yourself."

"Your personal integrity gets sanded away. You erode principles every day so you can live to erode another day. Sad, but true, friend. After a while you stop thinking about it and the numbness helps . . . sorta."

"So, yeah, we hear your words—and even agree with the sentiments. But we doubt the expediency of morality in this day and age."

I sit, stunned. "Expedient morality," I repeat the oxymoron half-aloud. I'm speechless. I sense the beating they've been taking and feel their defeat.

When they talked earlier (introduction) about the tough game of management, there was a hint of heroic competition in it that we could relate to. But this time, it's harder to identify with their comments even though we've all experienced the erosion of character they're talking about.

There's a voice in me that questions what they're saying. Something doesn't ring true here. These people are winners, they're successful. They're a sort of hero class. They're written about, quoted, powerful. By the standards used to evaluate life today, they're doing fine.

But think about those standards—that's where the untruth is. They're incomplete. Character is missing. Conspicuously. The standards we use to measure others, and thus live by ourselves, are all worldly, lower-self things like possessions and social status, even intellect. Character isn't even included! This phenomenon is seen graphically on the next page.

Yet character is the make-or-break ingredient that provides uniqueness and wholeness in life. Lack of character is a deficiency disease, a lack

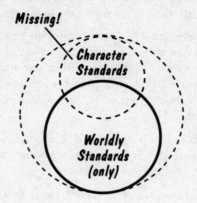

of the minimum daily requirement of the C vitamin. Whether or not people voice it or even think about it, they know that the absence of character means they're less than they were, less than they ought to be, and less than they were meant to be.

Handy Panel's truth hurts. But it isn't the only truth. There's a higher truth operating in integrity and dharma, to which we now turn.

WHAT IS INTEGRITY?

Integrity is having the courage and self-discipline to live by your inner truth. Imagine a human life lived that way. There's great honor in it.

It's not as distant or idealistic as we might think either. We've all had times during some era in our lives—a morning here, an afternoon there, and maybe, if we've been lucky, several days or weeks—when we've been able to live and act fully in concert with our own deep truth. It's a great feeling. My dream is to live life totally that way and to create that atmosphere in organizations.

There are five key ideas in that short definition of integrity: (1) wholeness and (2) goodness—both of those are implied in the word integrity—plus (3) courage, (4) self-discipline, and (5) living by inner truth. Let's touch on each:

1. *Wholeness* implies totality, soundness, perfection, and completeness—a sort of engineered structural integrity or strength. These ideas are appealing in our Western cultures. There is also a whiff of spiritual in wholeness—the implication being that we need to personally feel wholeness and perfection, and without Spirit, of course, we don't.

2. *Goodness* furnishes the honesty and morality we think of when we use the term *integrity*. Included in goodness are human decency, fairness, kindness, politeness, and respect. Described that way, integrity appears to be yet another face of love, which is a good indication that we're close to the heart of it. The root word "good" in *goodness* also implies quality, value, and worth. This deeper meaning of goodness is what the widespread "quality movement" in industry is all about. Goodness is what excellence is! Character and quality go hand in hand.

3. *Courage* isn't the absence of fear; it's proceeding in spite of it. Courage, in the business context, refers to little acts of valor, such as deciding not to hold back something you know needs to be said. It's telling the truth in the face of peril and pitfall. It's being candid when it may be dangerous. It's going ahead and doing it or saying it even if it's uncomfortable.

> Patrick, a consultant working with an apparently successful company, senses something is wrong. Despite the outward success, the atmosphere in the executive suite is flat and lifeless. How can this be?
>
> He talks with senior managers throughout the company trying to get a handle on the vanished vim. Slowly the answer pieces itself together: "creative bookkeeping." They have always lived a policy of going right up to the line of legality relative to taxes; recently they have tripped over that line a few times. Finding it so easy, they have taken up residence there, and it's sapping their vitality.
>
> What to do? Patrick knows the motivational project they hired him for won't work while this pall hangs over the place. He takes the weekend to mull it over, listening for directions from his inner truth.
>
> On Monday he walks into the president's office and recommends a full IRS audit. "A what?!!" Yes. He tells them for their own good to call in the Federal Revenuers. Is he out of his mind? What is this, Irish chutzpa? This advice all but empties the account of good will that he had built up with them.
>
> But this isn't only a story of Patrick's cheek. It's about leadership heart, too. After some heavy agonizing and

palpitations—and some good planning—the company
leaders decide to do it: they request an audit! It ends up
costing a few million dollars in back taxes and penalties.
Ouch! But vitality comes home—and creativity comes with
it. They soar again.

I once mentioned this story to the president of a large financial firm. His reaction was immediate. "Yeah, that was a smart move," his head bobbing forward as he said it, "not only honest but also practical!" He explained the dreadful drain of money, time, and spirit that double-dealing causes—and how all this casts a cloud over everything. His multimetaphored message: be brave, bite the bullet if you have to, and breathe the fresh air of integrity.

4. *Self-discipline,* the fourth key idea in integrity, is strengthening yourself to act in accordance with your inner promptings. This is discipline in the positive sense, not, as many people use the term, as punishment. Self-discipline is self-development. It's the cultivation of inner capabilities. It involves narrowing one's attention so it becomes a force that can be directed. Self-discipline is the stuff of good athletes. There's self-education, training, preparation, and practicing in self-discipline. It takes work.

You need both courage and self-discipline for integrity. Neither alone is sufficient. We all know courageous people who readily leap into the game but haven't got it sufficiently together to achieve goals. And we know highly disciplined people who, despite being organized, don't seem to have the nerve to make the leap. Integrity demands both.

5. *Living by inner truth* is most important of all. Inner truth communicates through faint whispers, thoughts, pictures, and feelings buried deep within us. Each and every human ever born on this planet possesses this truth and has the capacity to call it forth. It's a learned skill and it takes work. It's a rediscovery of one's subtle but true awareness.

You can't passively wait for inner truth; you must respectfully send for it. You need to continually turn inward, quietly, politely asking the right questions so that the subtle signals become clearer. What are the right questions? Each person has to ask his or her own, but for starters, here are four that can prime the pump:

Is this the way I want to live my life?

Is this the way I want to be treated?

Is this the way I want to treat others?

Is this action a turn toward or away from Spirit?

Then you turn inward, listen for answers, and proceed from there. Living by inner truth means putting truth into practice. It means holding yourself incorruptible and inviolable—no less than that.

"Incorruptible? Inviolable? In this world? Ha! Impossible!" we say. But think back. We've all had someone in our own lives who is an example of incorruptibility. Maybe that person wasn't perfect, nobody is. But somewhere in our experience is a model of character.

> Phil was the head purchasing agent for the first company I worked for. He was a white-haired, bulb-nosed, streetwise gentleman from Boston, much older than us recent MBA types. He wasn't fancy. His suits, with their wrong-width lapels, always hung rumpled on his stocky frame. Nevertheless, he was a wonderfully clear role model. He was responsible for buying perhaps a hundred million dollars worth of food and beverage items each year for the company. That part of the hospitality business is known for kickbacks, double-dealing, and shady behavior. People shrug it off and just don't think about it.
>
> But it wasn't in Phil to shrug. In the face of such corruption Phil squared his shoulders and was scrupulously, meticulously, impeccably honest. He wouldn't even take home one of the jillions of cocktail napkins or "free" ballpoint pens he bought for the company. Phil never even accepted a drink from the many sales reps who called him friend. "I'll drink with you, but I'll buy my own," he'd smile, pointedly.
>
> He didn't flaunt his integrity, but he always had the time to tell us how and why he was so careful about being that way, emphasizing personal impeccability. He taught us nose to nose, explaining until we understood—never a sermon, just friendly information. And he never tired of sharing this with the young people who passed his way.
>
> _____
>
> Also a while back I was privileged to spend time with Buckminster Fuller during the last couple years of his life. Bucky was a famed thinker-engineer-philosopher. He called himself a comprehensivist. Although he did not seem to have a creed in the usual sense, he was truly connected with spirit.

Louise was helping the Fuller Foundation plan a series of "Integrity Days"—massive workshops featuring Bucky and his ideas. I tagged along to her meetings with him as often as I could, because for years Bucky had been serving on my "Committee." This is a personal advisory board made up of heroes and role models, both living and dead (Ben Franklin, for example, is also on it). I had created it when I was a boy, the year my father died, to guide me through life.

Bucky didn't know of his membership on this august committee and I was too shy to tell him. It didn't matter anyway; he continued to serve well after I got to know him, and he still does. Bucky died at eighty-seven, a man of big vision and heart. His knowledge was far-reaching, but it was his integrity that most influenced the world—and me.

As a young married man, so the story goes, Bucky went into deep despair over the death of a beloved six-year-old daughter and a failed business in which he and his friends lost their money. He withdrew completely from the outer world. For two years he talked to no one, not a soul except wife Ann.

During the time spent in the depths of silence, he thought about many big life questions including whether he should go on living at all. Dark hours, deep quiet, and heavy queries are so often the basic recipe for enlightenment. The times we are most discouraged is when Spirit comes to us and provides guidance (depicted graphically on the next page).

Bucky eventually made a deliberate decision: yes, continue life, but only on his terms, and they were hard, disciplined terms that centered around basic integrity. One of his conditions, for example, was to live life for the good of humanity, not for personal aims. Another was that he would never talk to anyone unless invited. This meant he wouldn't impose his ideas or seek to get his views accepted or try to sway anyone one way or the other unless asked. Never being "on the make" is what it amounted to, exactly opposite from the world described by Handy Panel. Bucky meticulously lived that policy for the ensuing fifty-plus years of his life. He also became one of the most sought after university lecturers and guest speakers in the world.

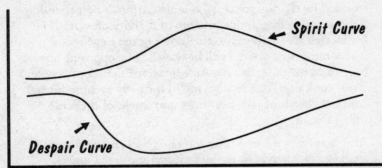

Adapted from *Life Changes* by Spencer and Adams 1990.

Phil and Bucky are examples of people who had the grit to live by inner truth. When I talk about living one's life that way, people take a quick breath and lean forward a little, eyebrows lift, "You mean it may be possible for me to do that?"

It may be more a daydream than a real question, but I answer anyway, "Not only possible, imperative." Then come the oblique questions about courage: "Isn't that dangerous? Isn't that impractical? How can you do that? How do you know what your inner truth is saying?" In other words, "Can I find the guts for this?"

The Specter of Faintheartedness

To answer these up-to-date pleas for intestinal fortitude, we reach back in time several millennia to the wisdom contained in the *Bhagavad Gita* ("The Song Celestial")(Mascaro 1971). The *Gita* is an epic, half-inch-thick Sanskrit poem in which the universal questions of life are posed and answered. Since it is packed with the secrets of living life well, the *Gita* naturally talks a lot about goodness, courage, and self-discipline.

I use this part of the *Gita* story often because it seems so pertinent to these times. Here it is:

> Arjuna, a great prince at the height of his powers, the greatest achiever and man of action of those times, is readying to go into battle. All his life he has been a courageous and successful warrior renowned for his prowess in combat. But this time, on the eve of the biggest clash of all, he begins to waver.

He's in his magnificent war chariot pulled by four white steeds. The chariot driver, who is also Arjuna's best friend, is Krishna, an avatar, an incarnation of divinity on earth. He has steered the chariot into the center of the huge moor where tomorrow's battle will be waged. The opposing armies have gathered on each side. An epic scene: masses of people, tents, cook fires, banners waving in the early evening breeze, conch shells blowing—the noises and smells of prebattle filling the air.

Arjuna surveys the opposing forces. He sees many former friends and relatives in the enemy camp: revered uncles, those who taught him his great warrior skills, all bravely making ready for tomorrow's clash. Arjuna slumps a little and looks at Krishna.

"Why am I doing this?" he asks. "This isn't right. Yonder are people to whom I should be paying earnest respect, but tomorrow I will be killing them. Life is so cruel and demanding. I don't know if I have the heart for this anymore." With that, his eyes fill with tears, he sinks to his knees, and he just gives up, saying something like, "What's it all about, Krishna, beloved friend? Please tell me."

A great moment. Can't you see it? This great warrior, slumped, pleading. And Krishna, totally calm, responds in effect, "Oh, so you really want to know? Okay." With that, he takes the next twenty minutes to give the answer—*the* answer! Straight from Source. Imagine! It's a fine example of what we were just talking about: Spirit coming to provide guidance at one of those darkest of times.

Remember the movie *Annie Hall* where the male character is standing in a theater line arguing some philosophical point from a Marshall McLuhan book? "Oh yeah?" he says and turns to a distinguished-looking man a few paces away, who just happens to be McLuhan. McLuhan, in no uncertain terms, gives the answer, straight from source.

Well, here we are, six thousand years ago with Arjuna, this great prince, this mighty warrior, brought to his knees by vast cosmic questions of life. He turns in desperation to ask his friend for the answer and his friend, who just happens to be the personification of all wisdom, gives it—straight from Source.

And what is "the answer"? My summary of it is: you can't *not* do your duty. That's right. No matter what your duty is in life, you must do it and do it well. Whether you're a professional or a sweeper or whatever—even a warrior—no matter what your particular role is, you must carry it out to the absolute limit of your human capacity for excellence. And the way to do this is to become established in higher self (that is, in Spirit). That is the place from which you perform your worldly actions.

Oh, the language of the *Gita* is majestic: "Yield not to unmanliness. Cast off this mean faintheartedness and arise, O scorcher of thine enemies." A little more stirring than my words, but people get what I mean.

The specter of faintheartedness reaches out to all of us sooner or later. The apparition of cosmic confrontation stalks us; the bearer of scorching life questions awaits us around the next bend. Eventually Arjuna's troubled state of mind comes to every soul. No escape. Some day the purposelessness of pomp, power, property, and pedigree comes at us with a force that brings us to us our knees, humble and reaching.

Arjuna's battle goes on inside us all. What are we really doing here and what does it all mean? The message: be a hero, not a goat, in life, in this greatest of all games. Do your duty! (Duty in the old-fashioned sense, as work, not as millstone.) Make virtue win!

You can't be a sheep and expect to gain any ground. Victory, especially inner winning, takes valor. Courage isn't just something we read about. It isn't something we possess or don't possess. Courage is a verb: it's something we do. Same with integrity, honesty, morality, internal truth, goodness—they're all things we do!

A TRUER LIFE

Now we return to the matter of living by inner truth. It isn't only the big, cosmic questions that knock us down. The lesser ones grind away almost unnoticed over time until our knees buckle and we start to wonder why. As Handy Panel said, people aren't big crooks. It's the petty things that slowly steal away our souls. Phil, the honest purchasing agent, knew that, which is why he was vigilant about even the tiniest incursion into his integrity.

It's not simply that people are dishonest. And it's not simply that they are nonspiritual. In fact, it's just the opposite. People are honest inside, and they are, as we've said, basically spiritual. It's that they've quit thinking about their honesty and have lost touch with their innate goodness.

They just never give it much thought, and they live in a society that doesn't give it much thought, and they work in human systems that don't provide support for living a more pure life. They're members of organizations that, passively or actively, contaminate people. People accept half-truths as just part of the game, and thus they condone them. And now they have a dim (or glaring) disquiet about whether they're whole.

That again is what the whole "Quality Movement" is about, and why the term *excellence* stirs so many people so deeply nowadays. That's why we're so touched when we hear of Isaac and other deeply caring leaders. The integrity issue is not only an effectiveness, nor even a survival issue—it's a spiritual issue.

CHAPTER 14

ADDING DHARMA: RIGHT ACTION, FEARLESSNESS, AND SPIRITUALITY

*Hidden away in the inner nature
of the real man is the law of his
life.*

—Ralph Waldo Emerson

For all intents and purposes, dharma and integrity are the same. People with real integrity are dharmic. We could use the terms interchangeably and get away with it except for three additions: Spirit, rightness, and fearlessness.

THE SPIRITUAL COMPONENT

Dharma stems directly from Spirit. It's rooted there. There's no shyness about spirituality in dharma—no reluctance, no separation. In that sense, dharma *is* Spirit.

On the other hand, integrity, rooted as it is in our fiercely secularized Western society, doesn't openly embrace spirituality. Despite the bounty of morality and incorruptibility that the notion of integrity brings, it only hints at Spirit through the idea of wholeness. That's not strong enough to register in the Western consciousness.

It's curious that integrity, which is often defined as wholeness, leaves out Spirit. People are bemoaning the "something missing" from their lives; yet Spirit, the piece of the puzzle that makes them whole, is left out!

It's that vacant-upstairs-room syndrome we met in Respiriting (part I). Spirit isn't home. The worldly lower floor is busy, noisy, overflowing with activity, but the upstairs is muffled, unused. The light is always on up there, but nobody's climbing the stairs. The passageway between the two floors might have been busy long ago—Spirit residing in the same house with integrity—but over the years it has been forgotten. Now the upper room is empty and the door hangs barely open, giving just a peek at what once lived there.

Then, dharma, with its blatant spirituality, flings the door wide, saying, "Do right, do good!" And the whole house is open, light, and complete again.

RIGHTNESS

Dharma is often translated from Sanskrit into English as "right action." The proverb *Dharma chara* means "do the right thing." The translation is okay but the Westerner, from a culture so oriented to action, naturally emphasizes the word *do* and tends to underemphasize the word *right*.

It's one of those subtle differences. You have to live within the idea of dharma for a while for the correct emphasis to come. Read it "*right* action" and "do the *right* thing" and the fine difference peeks through. The inner distinction is big. In dharma, *right*ness is the starting place, not do-ness. Doing right is more important than just doing.

FEARLESSNESS

There's another subtle difference between integrity and dharma that also arises from the contrast of West and East. Integrity calls for courage; dharma hails fearlessness. The same? Not really.

Courage, remember, is going ahead and doing something in spite of being afraid. Fearlessness is what it implies: no fear—it's an inner state that arises from profound spiritual knowing about the true nature of the Self.

The story of Alexander the Great's march into the Kulu Valley in northwestern India mythologizes the difference. Here's the mighty Grecian army with their spirited war horses, clattering along. They come upon a Yogi, a thin little man clothed in sackcloth, sitting cross-legged in the road.

They expect him to run, but he doesn't. The column halts.
He is ordered out of the way. He laughs. Alexander is called.
He rides up, brandishing his sword, threatening to lop off
the Yogi's head if he doesn't scamper.

The little man looks Alexander in the eye and laughs again.
Alex eyes him in return. There's something in the little man's
look and laugh—not defiance, just bone-deep congruence,
truth without a hint of fear. This is not a mere madman.

The great general scabbards his sword, turns to his officers,
and tells them it would be folly to invade a country of such
beings. The army turns and clanks back toward whence it
came.

If not mad, is the little man foolish or brave or what? None of those. It's
his fearlessness. He knows the Truth about himself at a core-deep, even
nucleus-deep level. He is solidly rooted in the wisdom that he truly is not
the body he inhabits—he's Spirit. Spirit is his true Self. And he knows just
as deeply that Spirit can't be "lopped off." Thus, he simply has no fear.
None! It's rare for most people (Westerners especially) to experience
fearlessness. We occasionally get glimpses of it, and we can conceptualize
it—but without being rooted in the beliefs, it's hard to imagine being
totally fearless.

INDIVIDUAL DHARMA

There's a personal-fit aspect of dharma. People talk as though each person
has his or her "own" dharma. "Follow your dharma," they say, or "Protect
your dharma and it will protect you." Personal dharma also applies to
particular groups: "They have to adhere to their dharma" is the way it's put.

This idea of exclusive dharma is the insight that shines through in
poet Emerson's line about "the inner law of one's life." Dharma is personal. It isn't a one-size-fits-all set of ethical standards. It's an inner formula
for only the individual. We each have our own law, or dharma, peculiar
to ourselves. It's as much a part of us as our body is, probably more.

As with any law, we have to comply with it or suffer the consequences.
Those times when we're unaware of or disregard that inner formula are the
times when we feel insufficient. That's the incompleteness people lament.
When we don't adhere to our dharma, our life comes apart. It veers
off course or gets stuck, or we become sick.

Leverage Magnifies Dharma

One's present station and level of achievement, or role in life, also affect one's dharma. An individual's dharma differs according to where he or she is in life. The dharma of the bank chairman, for example, is different from the dharma of the teller. This idea makes my egalitarian friends shudder.

It's not that the teller is lesser and the chairman more, it's just that they're in different places in life at this moment. This will change with time. For now, the differing responsibilities and leverage that each brings to the table of life earn each of them a distinct dharma.

My friend-client Joel, who, handily, just happens to be a bank chairman, often talks about "paying back." He's not referring to a loan; rather, he means the responsibility he feels to recompense the world for the gifts he has been given. "I owe!" he says, raising his eyebrows, seeming to draw strength from the two little words. What's shining through here is the inner law of his life. Complying with it makes Joel rich beyond the material things he owns.

ORGANIZATIONAL DHARMA

What's true for individuals is also true for collections of them. Of course dharma applies within the organization. There's a collective dharma, an organizational inner law—and each organization has its own.

The traits of courage, self-discipline, goodness, and doing right (emphasis on *right* again rather than *do*) are the marks of collective character, just as they are of individual character. Each organization must also follow its own collective heart and soul.

Management Dharma

And who do you think will get tagged with the responsibility for organizational character? Management—the people with the leverage.

There is a particular dharma for managers because they're in the responsibility seat. Their actions impact other humans and affect the economic and physical well-being of the organization and, beyond that, the well-being of the environment and even the planet. With that power comes a greater measure of accountability. Management dharma, like individual dharma, matches one's life station. Managers can't expect to take the bigger jobs and not take on a broader dharma.

The manager's dharma is more demanding, more obligated to rightness, and more careful (that is, more full of care). Banker friend Joel is right: managers do owe. Privilege isn't free. As was said: it is up to the manager to bring the power of character to the organization.

SPIRITUAL VALUES

Let's look at how this do-right-do-good, blatantly spiritual dharma plays out in organizations.

Jeff founded a financial services firm and grew it into an abundant jewel of a company. His formula: character. That's it. One word: character. He has a way of punching out the word *character* so you listen.

"Management has to accept responsibility for creation," he says. It's an interesting metaphor—creation—especially the way he uses it. He goes at it with zeal.

His one criterion for hire: character. He doesn't worry about defining it but knows it when he sees it. To show his commitment to it, he gets personally involved in the process of hiring all new people. The supervisors doing the hiring thus learn Jeff's definition and emphasis on character. The organization sprouts to over three hundred souls, all of them imbued with this emphasis.

Jeff sets the tone in other ways. Working with experts and consultants, he conducts training sessions for all employees. At the end of every day they go at it for two hours. That's every day, and everyone!

They cover the basic business topics, the "taking-care-of-knitting" things like sales figures and operating results. But beyond those, a set of Company Commandments is drawn up that gets heavy play in the sessions. These commandments spell out the moral behavior expected of all employees, in essence: don't lie, steal, or cheat, or else!

Each and every employee also participates in clarifying the company's basic purpose and essence: our primary aim is not to make money but to serve! They all get a chance to thrash this through and understand what that philosophy means to each of them in their jobs. This involvement develops a high commitment to service, which comes through to their clients.

Jeff installs a meditation room where people can sit and think, or just be. Sounds odd, and he takes some flak for it on the "Street," but he believes in the rightness of it. The room comes to symbolize the value of individual thinking in that organization. And, though not the original intention, many money-making ideas eventually come out of that quiet space.

Also, during training, employees draw pictures of their hopes and dreams for the organization. The pictures invariably depict a big, healthy, prosperous, generous, honest, happy, unified organization that's doing so great it's bursting at the seams. That image is replayed, reinforced, and thickened, over and over in everyone's mind. The what-you-think-about-you-bring-about principle proves true. This community of financial types who dream and draw pictures together flourishes.

Jeff says, "I discovered five or six years before founding the company that there's more to life than making money, or having possessions, or even family." In Jeff's case these words don't come out like cliches. He talks as if he knows a secret.

"All those things—money, position, goods, and even family—are 'worldly' things," he continues. "As important as they are, you have to go beyond them to spirit. That's why we're here on earth—it all boils down to materialism versus spirit." He says it in a way that leaves little doubt which side will win in his life.

For years the company is a Camelot in that money-driven industry. People not only make a lot of money but also they feel part of a community, they feel integrity. They love being there, and even hold back tears when they talk about it.

As I ruminate about the success of that organization and Jeff's almost yogic single-pointed dedication to character, I wonder if that's the answer. Can we directly link that company's achievement to the bigness of its character? Then, some doubt creeps in. Maybe it's the smallness of the organization— after all, just three hundred people.

But then I think of giant Matsushita with two hundred thousand more employees than Jeff's company. It's one of the world's largest companies: Panasonic, Quasar, Technics, and so on. Like any other company it has its ups and downs, but, like Jeff's organization, it is also a great place to be. Maybe it's not as intimate, but it is certainly successful and well-thought-of worldwide—and people like being there.

Matsushita also has a list of commandments. They call them their Seven Spiritual Values:

> National Service
>
> Fairness
>
> Harmony and Cooperation
>
> Struggle and Betterment
>
> Courtesy and Humility
>
> Adjustment and Assimilation
>
> Gratitude

Those values date back to the firm's founding over sixty years ago, and they still live. The late chairman of this sprawling organization was, like Jeff, single-minded about values. He referred to himself as "the soul of the company" and acted as the conduit and protector—the chief steward of the company's basic values. His choice of words reflects his inner truth.

Matsushita's values are embedded in the culture of the organization. Management works very hard nowadays to make sure all employees know and live by these precepts. It's all rather official. The preamble to the Spiritual Values statement is called the Employees' Creed. It spells out the importance of combined effort, and it prominently reminds people to continuously devote themselves to the improvement of the company.

That kind of devotion to a company creed might at first come across as rather ham-handed in other cultures, but it works there (and other cultures are picking it up). There are some beautiful gems embedded in Matsushita's creed. Hold the list of Spiritual Values up to the light:

> Within "National Service" is the idea of doing something bigger than oneself, of committing to something larger.
>
> In "Fairness" are the ideas of human justice, equity, and impartiality in dealings with people.

> In "Harmony and Cooperation" are inner peace, unity, and amity—qualities that everyone seeks.
>
> In "Struggle and Betterment" are the notions of accepting a less-than-perfect world, of playing the game well, of self-perfecting, and of heroism and winning.
>
> In "Courtesy and Humility" are the ideas of respect, dignity, decency, and egolessness.
>
> In "Adjustment and Assimilation" are selflessness, teamwork, and being one of the family.
>
> In "Gratitude" is tapped the immense personal power of appreciation.

Remember, these aren't from some textbook list of principles. They are the operating values, the moral policy of a huge, successful, modern organization.

Sometimes a yeah-but reaction is voiced. "Yeah but isn't that just a reflection of a homogeneous society or lifetime employment?" They just write it off; they rationalize away this goodness, this recipe for dharma.

In the States, a large organization that stands out as one of the most effective performers in the country also shares strong spiritual values even if they don't call them that. It's the U.S. Forest Service. "The jewel in the crown of the federal service," somebody called it. It is the only government organization on the list of "Cultures of the Future" in Deal and Kennedy's (1982) book *Corporate Cultures*.

And it is special. Spread all over the place—from tending the great bears in Alaska or the grizzlies in Montana to the "Smokey Bear" employees working in the suburbs of Los Angeles or Philadelphia—the Forest Service is, despite its diversity, amazingly coordinated and cohesive.

Whether the Forest Service people are tree cutters or preservers, bureaucrats in Washington or mountain men (and nowadays, women) in Colorado, they all have something terribly important in common: the land. Caring for the land is their spiritual glue. This love of the land is where the organizational character comes from. Regardless of pressure groups and politicians, buried in the collective soul of the Forest Service is its common cause: a caring for the land so deep it becomes reverence. The hushed-voice way they say "the land," you'd think they were in church.

CHAPTER 15

ENDOWING INDIVIDUAL AND ORGANIZATIONAL CHARACTER

> *Character is destiny.*
> —Greek proverb

> *There are no mountain peaks to climb. Just drop habits one by one.*
> —Sathya Sai Baba

Now that we've discussed integrity and dharma, we can tackle the concerns raised by Handy Panel (chapter 13). As you recall, they didn't just shed light on things; instead, they directed the glare smack in our faces. Suddenly we're squinting into their description of the harsh reality of life suffered by managers nowadays:

> How do we live a right life in a world that tears at our integrity?
>
> How do we protect our humanness, our caring?
>
> How do we harden ourselves against compromise?
>
> How do we scrub away the deceit and self-interest that stick to us in organizations?
>
> How can we stop sandpapering truth?
>
> How can we guard our values in the hard, real world?
>
> How can we muster the courage to push back against all this?

They're hard questions and, as Handy Panel said, they're seldom voiced. As I travel through the management world, I hear them in the cracks between other topics, such as how one manipulates to get things done. I hear them echoing behind schemes for making people "feel" that they have a say in things when they really don't. I hear them discussed over dinner, after the so-called real work is finished and we're just visiting.

I hear those questions from people "in trouble" in the system, who can't, or won't, master the skills to live in it. I hear them from people who, now that they have "made it," are saying, "Is this all there is?!" And I hear those questions in my heart for people whose anguish I observe as they undergo the day-to-day erosion of self.

GETTING INTO THE SPIRIT AND HABIT OF CHARACTER

Art, my football coach, used to say, "You're never *in* physical shape, you're either going in one direction or the other, into better or worse shape." It's the same with character. You're always going one way or the other. It's not just "set it and forget it"; you have to work toward a better character.

Perhaps a more poetic way of saying it is that in the inner, inner heart of character is heart. When you get that deep, or high, there's light—it's an experience of brightness. That light grants power to character. Moving into that radiance is what recharactering is really about.

Fourteen How-Tos for Assigning Character

So how can you move into that radiance and get into better character? Here are fourteen examples of strategies, tactics, mental states, attitudes, postures, and routines that help individuals and organizations do their recharactering:

1. *In the System, Yet Not the System.* Although you may be a fragment of the system, you're not the system. And you are especially not a part of the dishonesty or meanness in the system. Deliberately detach your mind from the badness and adhere only to the goodness in the system.

2. *Personal Might, Organizational Power.* When you have to go against the system, be bold, be brave, be firm, be friendly, be wise—and be careful. Take it step-by-step, and step smartly, from a platform of personal power. People think they are weak and the system is strong, but it's usually the opposite. The reason organizations are often protective and rigid is not because they're so strong (that kind of behavior doesn't derive

from strength); it's because they're so fragile.

This perspective brings wisdom and strength. My friend Ken was an inspiration. He was able to perform excellently and stay fully alive in a huge, stifling bureaucracy—and maintain a lifelong integrity despite the prudence, shrewdness, caution, and canniness inherent in large organizations. His secret? Through thick and thin he remained hooked to his own inner truth and drew his okayness from within himself. Thus, he was never far from the higher part of himself, and this strengthened him in the lonely times when the system pressured him to buckle. Ken wasn't what he would call religious, but he was a spiritual man.

3. *Personal Credo.* The greatest decisions of life are made daily in the silent inner garden of the soul. Cultivate and nurture that private place. Draw up a personal manifesto that reflects the light and goodness of your own ethics and morality. Be deliberate about it. Make it a part of your personal mission statement. Use it as a life policy, as clear directions from the top—which isn't "up there" somewhere but is in you. Anchor your daily actions in this credo. Make your life fit your own principles. Be right with life. That's what dharma is.

4. *The Power of Acceptance.* Most people don't get into the habit of affirming, acknowledging, or embracing life. Thus, they never feel affirmed, acknowledged, or embraced by life.

Too bad, because acceptance frees the energy that gets tied up in feeling hurt or frustrated. It's like neighbor Al's coming to terms with his illness (chapter 2). When he finally accepted it, including his coming death, his scant energy expanded outward to help him get well. And it brought him great peace of mind. Healers teach us that all healing begins with acceptance.

Being angry and frustrated about something (or someone) gives your power away to that. But acknowledging it and granting it pardon brings an ease with it—and then power swoops back. This isn't resignation; rather, it's our capacity to just accept things as they are, it's our capacity for truth.

Acceptance is an attitude. It's a mood, a mental state. It's one's general policy on relating to the world at large. And it's a verb—an active reaching out and approving the way things are. It's saying yes, yes, yes to life.

"Acceptance is a face of love," says consultant-writer Harrison Owen (1991). So we're again dipping into the reservoir of strength called love. As we know, go deeply enough into any of these issues and you arrive here, at love. It's coming home again.

5. *Be the Boss.* Hard, tough decisions still have to be made. You're accountable. You have to be the boss. Trying to be "nice" probably won't work (cream puffs may be sweet at first, but ultimately they're sickening). Just do those boss things from inner truth, do them in a dharmic way, with integrity. Do your job, but don't ever violate character, ever. Character must *always* come out on top.

6. *Inner Listening.* Inner truth is the distilled essence of character. Integrity, after all, is but living by inner truth. Dharma and integrity exist only by their connection to inner truth. Call it conscience, perceptiveness, discernment, or whatever—it behooves us to call it, and listen to it. How listen? Adjust your antennae in that direction. There's a science associated with listening to inner voice, but the method of discovery in it is different from regular science. The whole point is to go inside, not outside, for the data.

There are five keys to inner listening: Quiet, Believe, Ask, Listen, and Trust (Q-B-A-L-T). Let's touch on each:

Quiet

How turn inward? First, be quiet. People have their own modus for inner listening. Sometimes they're not even aware of doing it, but all the methods start with becoming still.

"Start with quiet" was my answer to a group of doctors who asked me how to meditate. Not just meditation, no matter what you're trying to do—whether it's healing, acting, sports, growing, loving—whatever it is, it begins with the pacific; it starts with quieting inner commotion. In the stillness is the power.

The problem is there's a constant hustle-bustle going on in our heads. We're always thinking, thinking, thinking. It's a wild, busy scene in the dome. In the East they dub this a "mad (or drunken, or scorpion-stung) monkey." Disciplining such an animal is not easy.

The mind-discipline drill is called various names: concentration, quiet sitting, relaxation, focusing, contemplation, musing, receptive meditation, yoga. But basically it's quiet. No quiet, no truth.

How become quiet? Just sitting and shutting your eyes is a good start. The mind appreciates quiet and will seek it if given a chance. Maybe peaceful walking, knitting, or even jogging can do it for some people, but most people have to be still to be quiet. Blessed quiet—that's when faint signals can come from within.

The aim is to still the mind, to stop thinking. How? Some do it by becoming aware of breathing—counting or watching breaths. Others do it by relaxing their muscles one by one. Another common way is to repeat a pleasant sound or name over and over for several minutes, or even several hours, or days. (Recall the repetition of "*Aumsairam,* yes" in chapter 3.) There are myriad other ways to call forth quiet, and they're all good.

The idea is to effortlessly focus your attention on itself, being advertent to your own awareness, bringing your attention inside. You can't force it, it's a nondoing. It's an unhooking from external, worldly activities, while circling one's energy back to where it comes from.

Believe

The key to inner listening is (again) *believing* in it. Whether inner truth surfaces depends on whether you believe it will, and whether you believe that what you will hear will be useful and true—and whether you welcome it. How often you receive inner signals is also related to how much you believe in them. The more you believe, the more reception capacity you have.

Ask

It is up to us. We have to initiate the process. First ask, then allow yourself to receive. And put the question respectfully, even lovingly, as though talking to a powerful old friend. "Please, [Inner Truth], give me a symbol or message about . . . (whatever)." Or, "Please help me phrase the right question." Putting forth the right question is important.

Along the way it's also important to release, to let go of it, to stop trying for inner guidance. Why? Because the act of trying gets us thinking, and thinking is not very useful in this process. Releasing is often what beings the message. It doesn't seem logical, but people know it works. The act of letting go is what provides room for the answer to come. So be deliberate: explicitly, clearly, sincerely, and vividly request, and then definitely release.

Ask often. Make the time and space in your life to talk to your inner self as regularly as possible—daily, several times a day. Practice might not make perfect, but it makes it habitual; the aim, remember, is to develop a good habit.

Listen

Listening is more than auditory reception. Messages come in words, symbols, feelings, physical or metaphysical (that is, beyond physical) reactions, or in combinations thereof. The messages might be visual, verbal, vibrational, or something else. And they come when it's their time—when the time is right—which could be, and often is, quite soon, but perhaps not immediately when beckoned. Sometimes, they're faint and need to be amplified; other times, they're indirect and you need to decipher and interpret them.

But all this doesn't take a medium or clairvoyant. Inner listening is simpler than we make it. If you want to receive then, well, be receptive. As simple as that. And be patient. Inner listening isn't a matter of what you actually do or don't do, it's more a function of what your attitude is.

Trust

Don't expect the messages to be notarized and delivered by certified mail. They come in vague ways. We have to trust the signals, in whatever form they arrive. Trust has elements of faith, confidence, and obligation in it. It means not only receiving the signals but also putting them into practice. It means relying on them more in life so that your inner dictates become clearer and are always with you.

It's like constant spiritual awareness. You first make yourself aware of inner voice, then you encourage its around-the-clock participation. Listening to one's inner truth *is* being whole—it *is* integrity, *is* dharma.

7. **Do No Harm.** "Good, Clever, Cunning, Cagey, and Guile"— sounds like a law firm, but it's not. They're stops along the character-to-chicanery continuum (see figure on following page). We all range up and down that street as we live our lives and do our jobs. We have to if we're functioning and getting things done.

Read those signboards. It's not a clear-cut matter of choosing light over darkness. We'd all always make the right choice if that were the case. Sometimes we have to be clever, or even cunning, to achieve our ends. And some situations seem to require cageyness, or even guile. Fact is, it's not simple. There are choices to make along the way. In life we pick from a array of behaviors.

The point is to never go so far that it harms others or yourself. The key word here is *harm* because that spot is where the violation of character occurs.

As you range along the continuum, be aware (and beware). When it doesn't feel right, stop; leave that place and back down the street until it feels okay again. Never go even a little beyond your own sense of rightness—wherever it may be along the continuum—because that sense is inner truth calling.

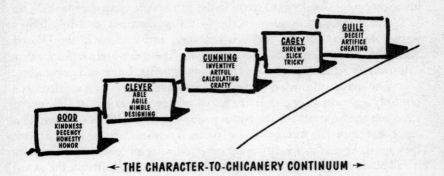

← THE CHARACTER-TO-CHICANERY CONTINUUM →

8. *Always Pay.* This is another of Sai Baba's little rules of life that seems simple but holds great significance. "Always pay" doesn't refer to paying your bills or cutting up our credit cards. It refers to a state of mind, a life policy of no debts, mental or material. It advises us to be unbeholden to anyone or anything, and thus be ever strong. It's a spiritual-warrior posture. Carry no arrears; owe nobody nothing. Ever.

9. *Love It, Change It, or Leave It.* Don't stay stuck. Hanging around and blaming the system for your gloominess is making your happiness depend on how the organization treats you. That's giving your power over to the organization. Don't.

On the one hand, choose to accept, opt for the healing that comes with acceptance. On the other hand, choose to wage change on the system to the point where you can begin to accept it. If neither hand works, dust them off—clap, clap—and move to a different organization or another company.

If it's an extreme case, you can pull out of the system entirely and build a different life. You don't have to go along with the system. You can be your own person. But beware of running away. Sometimes it works; often it's just a ruse to duck reality. Solutions aren't to be discovered in the backwoods, they're in us—in our hearts and spirits.

10. *Ceiling on Desires.* Are you feeling trapped in the pursuit of possessions, owned by the things you own? You're suffering from the common disease of "More." And you know by now that more is never enough.

Example: executive compensation in America. A blue-ribbon commission, of Nobel Prize economists and other experts, convened at MIT (long before that issue got in the media) and found absolutely no justification for the skyward trend in the pay of American executives. The U.S. industry's performance in the world marketplace certainly hasn't warranted it; yet the gap between managers and workers in the United States, and between U.S. executives and their counterparts in other countries, is exploding. It makes no business sense, but greed never does.

Endless consumption is a hunger that gnaws even when satisfied. It's not only a national condition, it's also a worldwide addiction. The greed steed has the bit in its mouth and is galloping away with our planet. The more that countries and the people in them consume, the more they think they need. Yesterday's luxuries become today's entitlements. Eventually it's all but impossible to ratchet back to less consumption. People the world over are working to maintain their overblown buying habits. Even third world countries are racing to leap on the back of the beast.

A well-known economist guest lecturing on this problem at the ashram university refers to Sai Baba's "Ceiling on Desires" program and nods his scholarly head at the elegant simplicity of it. "It's so uncomplicated it almost slips past, but that's the answer," he states in his British public school accent. "Economists may call it demand management, but ceiling on desires is the spirit of it."

So cap your cravings, ice your indulgences, and hem in your hankerings. All desires, as we have learned, including even satisfied ones, just add more hunger. Unless you tame them, they consume you.

11. *Empower Purity.* When you feel contaminated (and you're the one who must make this call), you have to scrub up—and the sooner the better even if it isn't a major thing causing it. Contamination doesn't just sit, it accumulates. You're getting either cleaner or dirtier.

How do you decontaminate? Reprogram yourself. Someone orders you not to think of an elephant when you take an aspirin, and what happens? The next time you toss a tablet, Dumbo flies into your mind. Why? You were programmed.

Use the same mechanism to program purity (or call it truth, or honesty, or whatever). Have purity supersede the contaminants. How do you do that? Fixate on purity. What we continuously put our attention on is what we eventually become.

Reprogramming may sound ordinary, but it's the basic substance of personal transformation (which is basically what recharactering is). Repeat: this is what life is for—the gradual reawakening to our inner goodness. It's what the ancients in India call *Sadhana* (pathway). Reprogramming is asking one's resident higher self for help. It's a variation of inner listening. In the case of contamination, we reprogram to call forth innate purity.

You don't just think about purity. You think it, feel it in your heart and body, touch it, talk to it and about it, see it in living color, even smell it. You go to bed and dream of it, wake up and have it before coffee. Vivid inner dialoguing about being pure is what it takes. Remember, "As felt, so fashioned."

The aim of all this? Power. Empower your purity (your truth, honesty, and so on) so it can empower you. Bringing purity so cleanly into consciousness makes that truth the strongest part of you. Strengthening, uplifting oneself is the goal.

And make it automatic. Do this reprogramming each time you feel you are being corrupted; it not only gives you a ride out of the bad situation, it becomes a habit. It's a good habit dislodging a bad one. It's another example of energy being used to change energy. It's not internal warfare though; it's an orderly substitution of purity rather than a brawling eviction of contamination.

Become practiced at it and an amazing thing happens: contamination begins to serve as a reminder of its opposite! When occasions arise that might corrupt, internal circuits automatically switch over to the purity program. Purity then becomes self-enacting.

12. *Think Character.* We've heard over and over that people "just don't think." Well, No-Think is also an automatic program. When something comes up that's against one's character, No-Think switches on. (It's also called defensiveness and avoidance.) Why not replace it with a better one: Character-Think, for example? The more you think character—and talk, visualize, smell it—the more power you imbue it with.

13. *Regrow Wholeness.* Make yourself whole again. Whatever you lost—openness, heart, courage, purity—grow it back. It will take persistence. It requires planning, strategizing, and maybe even a little conniving. It make take a while, that's okay, the loss didn't happen overnight. There really are no mountains to climb, just habits to drop one by one. Slowly and surely reclaim, refill, and become whole—and thus regain your Self.

14. *Rx for Recharactering Human Systems.* When the character of the organization needs work, whether simple tune-up or major overhaul, it's your lot as a manager to get that repair work done. If you're not a manager, these prescriptions pertain as well to one's personal recharactering within an organization. It's a new clause in your position description: metaresponsibility for organizational (or personal) character.

If not you, who? The obligation comes with the territory. When you donned the robe of management, you assumed the broader dharma. This is your chance to add light to the sum of light, to move the system toward its higher self. It's a spiritual orientation. No less is needed nowadays.

You recharacter your organization by: (a) taking the lead yourself, (b) being crystal clear about organization values and integrity, (c) granting space and voice so that others can arrive at clarity on ethical standards, and (d) actually *conferring* character. Consider each of the four:

Taking the Lead Yourself

First, you have to model personal integrity and then you have to demand it. There's no other way. The character of an organization is leader-bound. Any process to strengthen it won't work without the boss. You're either part of the solution or part of the problem. You have to know your own values and live by them impeccably—and do it openly so that others will emulate you.

Even if you're not at the top of the whole organization, you're at the top of your particular segment—division, zone, department, section, or wherever. You work character from the top down in your own organization from whatever level that "top" happens to be.

Being Crystal Clear

Send crisp signals from the top. The boss must do the pronouncing. "This, b'god, is what we stand for!" The following (from James Autry [1991], ex-CEO, Meredith Corporation's magazine group) is an example of a corporate values statement that sends that message:

> *We will be fair, sensitive, honest, trusting, and trustworthy in all our dealings among ourselves, with customers, with vendors, and with the community at large. We will obey all laws, in fact and in spirit, and we will always do the right thing, in every situation, to the best of our abilities. And if we fail, we will do whatever is required to make amends.*

Granting Space and Voice

"Integrity is an interactive event," say Srivastva and Associates (1988) in *Executive Integrity*. Dialogue is the operative soul of the human system with integrity.

Being clear about organizational values and morals is easy at the level of principles but harder the closer you get to having to operate by them. The practical issue of clarifying and implementing such principles in day-to-day practice is where the leader has to enable others.

People need a forum for private discussion of integrity dilemmas in their work. They need a place where they can talk with one another about their own special questions of integrity. The absence of such a forum is the cause of the moral stress felt by people in organizations.

Managers have to create the occasions for these forums. Look at them not as a formal program but as semiformal character chats, as events for moral dialogue. Management professor James Waters (in Srivastva and Associates 1988) calls them "Good Conversation," in which clear ethical positions can emerge through straightforward exchange and healthy debate. Some guidelines for moral dialogues are set forth on the following page. Moral dialogues are times for getting concerns and dilemmas out in the open and obtaining the views, advice, and support of others. They're not a reversion to starched Victorianism, but a way to learn, to clarify, and feel less lonely.

The moral dialogue process is rather unfamiliar and difficult to get started; it requires deliberate attention. It takes some practice to refine and improve it. People need to get into the habit of talking about these sorts of things. The key to success lies in the spirit behind these dialogue occasions. Leaders, as we said, have to take responsibility for their conception and their success, and this is not done by magic. Here's an example reported by Badaracco and Ellsworth (1989):

> James Burke, CEO at Johnson & Johnson, became con-
> cerned a few years ago that managers were treating the
> company credo with tokenism. He called a special meeting of
> twenty top managers. "Here's the credo," he began. "If we're
> not gong to live by it, let's tear it off the wall." It wasn't
> comfortable, but it led to a spirited discussion of company
> values and the individual managers' own personal values.
> Burke felt so good about the conversation that he continued
> to meet with groups of managers all over the world to simi-
> larly challenge and repeatedly reinforce the credo.

Conferring Character

The manager-leader's task is nothing less than conferring dharma and integrity. Sounds audacious at first: "conferring" character as though it can

Moral Dialogue Guidelines

❑ Special, not just business as usual

❑ Scheduled, staffed, and sustained

❑ Informal but intentional, designed so that real issues are uncovered and discussed openly

❑ Not theory or education

❑ True dialogue among equals, not boss-subordinate or teacher-student tone; dissent *must* be legitimate

❑ Inclusive of the power hierarchy

❑ As close to real-time operations as possible

❑ Mainstream, not handed over to a staff group

❑ Built into the performance and operations review processes that already occur in the organization

❑ Ongoing and deliberate, not just "as needed," or they won't happen

just be bestowed upon a human system. Well, to get on with it, the manager must assume that it *can* indeed just be conferred—and must assume that it is his or her responsibility to do the assigning of character.

Human-system recharactering isn't just a "mode of operating"; rather, it's an attitude, a mood, a way of being. It's based on an inner knowing of what's right and good—and trusting that intuitive knowing. It's a leap, a paradigm shift.

You *endow* your people with heart and grit to live by integrity. You literally "in-courage" them. You *grant* fearlessness, wholeness, and goodness. You *require* self-discipline. You *expect* adamantly and openly that the organization live as closely as humanly possible by its collective inner truth. All this is beyond the usual management job—it's superb management, it's spiritual leadership.

This is where the wizard in you comes into play. It is you, the manager-leader, who has to guide the voyage to the inner heart. You are the one to bring this power. You are the lighter of this lamp.

PART V

REINSPIRING

THE SPIRITUAL CORE OF LEADERSHIP

This section ranges beyond management to examine the roles of leadership and their spiritual core. Our discussion of management and leadership ends in the presence of a remarkable old king who provides some hard lessons about being a leader.

CHAPTER 16

ALL LEADERSHIP IS SPIRITUAL

The ancient tribal peoples who wandered thousands of years ago in the lands that later became known as Phoenicia always carried a long, straight tree trunk with them. This was a valuable possession. When they made their new home, the leaders would have the pole placed solidly into the ground, signifying that place to be the very center of the universe. People felt better living there, anchored deep into the earth and touching also the heavens, thereby connected to both.

Let's follow the tracks from good management onward to get a closer look at leadership, and then go further into the spiritual basis of it.

For generations we have honed management techniques without paying much attention to leadership. But over the past decade or so, the growing examination of real leadership has made it painfully clear that much of our sophisticated management isn't working in today's world. We now need more than just expanded and enhanced management. Trying to do what we usually do—bear down harder and do more management—isn't going to work. We have to reach past even superb management. We have to allow the new paradigm.

The new model—which we call the management/spiritual leadership model—tells us that the functions of managers and leaders are different, and that the very basis of leadership is spiritual. This doesn't mean management is no longer legitimate, noble, or needed. In fact, it's all those and more so—we've never been more in need of good, solid management. Without good management, organizations simply don't work.

However, this new model (as illustrated on the next page) does mean that the two roles are quite distinct. Leadership comes from a further, more spiritual place than good management. To mark this distinction, let's look at the model in its comparison of management and leadership. It lays out key functions, interests, and concerns of managers, and it extends that list to roughly comparable concerns and interests of leaders. Then, it takes that further, into the spiritual basis of leadership and the roles of spiritual leaders.

Compare across the lists and you get a good idea of the reach. Managers are concerned with goals and objectives; leaders are concerned with vision. Managers are interested in honesty; leaders are interested in integrity. Managers work with priorities; leaders are stewards of basic values. Managers create plans and strategies; leaders effect and maintain a state of mind. Managers are fundamentally "getters" (of budget, staff, and so forth); whereas leaders are the opposite, they're basically givers (of their vision, values, gratitude, and so on). Once this sinks in—that they are to *give* rather than acquire—the whole game changes.

Continuing, we see that good management, as we've long known, is "people management," the management of human effort; but leaders work at the more abstract level of people's energy, heart, and spirit. We also see that managers deal in organization form and teamwork (structures and systems for doing the work); whereas leaders deal in organization culture and a sense of community.

We note that management, to a large extent, is the evaluation and correction of performance; while leadership is more a matter of acknowledging and appreciating contributions. And finally, we see that managers are essentially in the business of problem solving and decision making; whereas leaders are in the business of establishing a stature or presence that makes their influence, guidance, and values felt throughout the organization whether or not these leaders are physically present.

The Management/Spiritual Leadership Model

The Functions, Interests, and Concerns
of Management and Leadership
—and Their Spiritual Basis

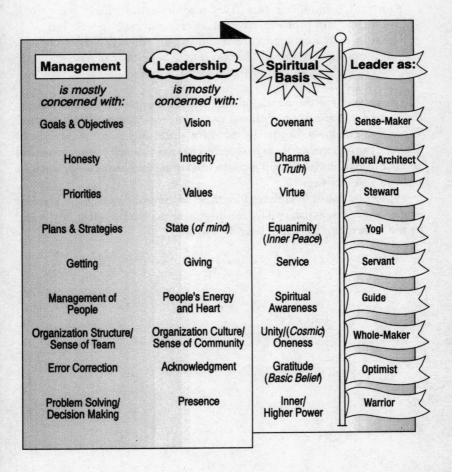

Management is mostly concerned with:	Leadership is mostly concerned with:	Spiritual Basis	Leader as:
Goals & Objectives	Vision	Covenant	Sense-Maker
Honesty	Integrity	Dharma (*Truth*)	Moral Architect
Priorities	Values	Virtue	Steward
Plans & Strategies	State (*of mind*)	Equanimity (*Inner Peace*)	Yogi
Getting	Giving	Service	Servant
Management of People	People's Energy and Heart	Spiritual Awareness	Guide
Organization Structure/ Sense of Team	Organization Culture/ Sense of Community	Unity/(*Cosmic*) Oneness	Whole-Maker
Error Correction	Acknowledgment	Gratitude (*Basic Belief*)	Optimist
Problem Solving/ Decision Making	Presence	Inner/ Higher Power	Warrior

The new CEO and top executives of a huge, closely controlled company meet to discuss ways of making the organization more flexible and competitive. The consultant notices they're using *management* and *leadership* interchangeably; therefore he shifts the discussion onto the distinctions between the two. As the group talks, lists of functions and concerns similar to those in the model emerge and are recorded on the chalkboard.

At the end of the discussion one of the key executives leans forward, rubbing his chin. "Hey, read down those lists," he observes, "our problem isn't that we're not managing well, but that we're managing too much and leading too little!" The rest of the group sits, thunderstruck. It's the beginning of a new way of looking at their top-management roles.

The same goes for thousands of thunderstruck organizations nowadays: the top people are too big on management, too skimpy on leadership. When we read down the management and leadership lists, the differences between the two spring out at us. Management, in a word or two, is control and coordination; leadership is profound caring and respect—you might say love and spirit.

Just how basically different are these two sets of functions? If you live by the management list, you'll probably have a successful career. If you live by the leadership list, you'll have a good life.

CHAPTER 17

THE ROLES AND PRACTICES
OF SPIRITUAL LEADERSHIP

Let's now leave management-leadership comparisons to delve into some of the key truths, powers, and practices of spiritual leaders.

▷COVENANT: LEADER AS SENSE-MAKER

The leader's first task is to define reality, to make sense of the organization and its environment. As leader, you need a personal, overall concept of the organization: what it means, why it is in business, what its great purpose is, and what kind of place you want it to be. It all begins with you, as the leader, first clarifying the agreements you've made with yourself, with the universe within. That act sustains all that follows.

Heeding one's inner knowing is at the center of real leadership and at the center of everything in this book. When leaders follow their hearts—as, for example, Isaac of the Hard Rock Cafe did (chapter 5)—others rise to those heights. This aspect of leadership comes from higher self. You follow your dreams for the organization, and you muster the courage to share them. You trust inner truth enough to allow your ideals to steer your life.

As the sense-maker, you have to look into the company's state of mind to learn of the hopes and dreams of the people in the organization;

and you have to examine the business environment to discern what rings true for the company. Then, you overlay your own ideals and values, and stir. This admixture is brought forth as a superordinate goal echoing both the aspirations of the work force and the requirements of the marketplace.

A basic bargain is struck in the hearts, minds, and spirits of the people. This is what makes it all feel right and good; it provides a general sense of sanction and endorsement at the core of things. This is what *meaning* is. People are hungry for it; without it, they weaken and flounder.

This is what makes you a sense-maker. In a way, you're privy to the universe's plans; you're cocreator of the universe (or at least your segment of it); you're a signer of a sacred covenant. You're a recipient of a cosmic handshake. Your feet are planted in the earthly, but you reach beyond, connecting both.

You bestow an awareness of something larger than ordinary life. This is the core of spiritual leadership, this grand gift, this feeding of people's hunger for Spirit. It's an act of love and creation, a tapping into the mysterious reservoir of human spirit, energy, and creativity.

The metaphor often used (and overused) with leadership is "vision." As a leader, you bring your vision to the workplace and, very important, you allow others to bring theirs. You share your insight, foresight, and farsightedness; and you enable others to pursue their own special sightings. You use disciplined imagination to see, read, hear, and feel the company's greater destiny—and you set it up so others do the same.

Visioning may appear more dreamy than achieving concrete management objectives, but it's often far more important. A grand and possible vision can bring a genuine sense of purpose, and that purpose feeds our craving for something bigger than ourselves.

Leadership visions aren't erected, they're detected. Another kind of knowing is involved. Bucky Fuller talked of visioning as "cosmic fishing." Vision comes from dipping your line into the vastness of universal truth. It is Spirit that furnishes the truth in vision and breathes life into it.

While true vision may be born of the gods in heaven, it also springs from more earthly wells. Listening well within the organization and staying well attuned to customers and the environment is also a source of vision. This broad attunement feeds intuition, and intuitive managers are always well-informed managers.

A number of years ago I was influenced by Roger Harrison's (1983) work in strategic planning. Here are some questions that I've since adapted to invite vision.

Vision-Call Questions

☐   By and large, are we living our inner truth?

☐   What are we called to do?

☐   What needs in the world are we moved to meet?

☐   Who are we?

☐   What are our gifts?

☐   What are our distinctive competencies?

☐   What do we have to contribute that's unique?

☐   What special knowledge do we have?

☐   What should we be especially grateful for?

☐   What do we value?

☐   What do we believe in?

☐   What do we do when we're really up against it?

☐   What activities have "heart" for us?

☐   What do we love doing?

☐   What does our environment need from us?

☐   What do we need from our environment?

☐   How *can* we break through to our next level?

▭ SERVICE: LEADER AS SERVANT

> *You care a lot and give a lot.*
> —Louise Hawley

Good management is the act of getting, getting the most out of people: more budget, more profit, more productivity. The management mind-set, correctly, is to get something for everything that you give. Leadership, on the other hand, is an act of *giving*. This is the great secret in great leadership. Giving is a sea change in the way managers think, act, and are. This is the difference between managers and leaders. This is the difference that makes a difference, a difference at the level of being.

Giving what? Just *giving*. Giving as a way of life. Giving whatever the situation needs—the vision talked of above, for example. Giving yourself. Giving others the freedom to pursue their dreams. It's the sharing of personal values, imparting the sense that everything makes sense, giving heart-deep support for human dignity and excellence, awarding "medals" for valor on the job. These are the boons that good leaders set forth.

There's a catch, however: you have to give with no strings attached and no deal in mind. Real leadership is not bartering; it's giving. The very basis of it is selflessness.

There's an added aspect of giving worth mentioning here, a universal absolute that's at play in giving. It's another of those sure rules of life that we know but sometimes forget we know: it's the Give:Get Ratio. Simply put, you get what you give. Always. Period.

In biblical terms, it's you reap what you sow; in Eastern thought, it's your *karma*. All cultures and societies on the planet have their counterparts of this principle. We all know at some level that what comes to us is in some way connected, maybe even reciprocal, to what we send out.

And this staunch rule never sleeps; it's always operating, including in business organizations. Workers always give to the organization or firm in direct proportion to what they perceive themselves receiving from it. Leaders need to be aware of this. When higher-ups bemoan the lack of worker commitment to the organization, I challenge them to examine the company's commitment to the workers. When they question worker loyalty, I raise questions about how loyal the company is toward its workers.

Generally, what we're talking about relative to this giving principle is the creation of an overall aura of giving. Giving comes naturally when you care deeply. It's another face of love, and that makes spiritual leadership an act of love. It's that simple (again).

▭ SPIRITUAL AWARENESS: LEADER AS GUIDE

> *Spirituality is a condition of*
> *utmost simplicity costing not less*
> *than everything.*
>
> —T. S. Eliot
> (paraphrased)

Good leaders are ceaselessly, invariably, regularly aware of Spirit. And all true leadership is spiritual because the leader seeks to liberate the best in people, and the best is always linked to one's higher self. Therefore it involves the creation of a collective state of constant spiritual awareness, a continual fusing of high things with the worldly.

Many say that good management is "people management." Leaders, however, don't just manage people; leaders learn to work at the more abstract level of spirit, energy, and so forth. Thus, leaders traffic in the mysteries of zest recovery; and to do their job, they learn to rely on the vast forces living in the ethereal idea of love. It is at this transcendent altitude that they live and work. It means reaching higher.

Consultant Jim Ritscher (1992) talks of "inspired leadership that creates upliftment." He's referring to leadership at its best, when it takes your breath away, and gives new breath—when it takes you into that higher circle, that upper room. In this sense, as we've seen throughout this book, great leadership is an energy source for the organization.

▭ UNITY/(COSMIC) ONENESS:
LEADER AS WHOLE-MAKER

> *The key to the ninety-nine is the*
> *one . . . how you treat the one*
> *reveals how you regard the ninety-*
> *nine because everyone is*
> *ultimately one.*
>
> —S. Covey

> *The only way to achieve Unity*
> *amidst all this diversity is through*
> *spirituality.*
>
> —Sathya Sai Baba

At some level, good leaders know about Unity and bring it to their organizations. It's a reuniting with the old, old truth of basic oneness. This is the deepest spiritual truth. We know in some faraway, long-forgotten chamber of our being that we are indeed not divided. We're aware of a oneness that is at once unfathomable and yet undeniable.

At the intellectual level, it stems from our knowledge that we're all bits of the same stuff, hurled into eventual life from the same big bang seventeen billion years past. Thus our connectedness is indeed cosmic. We're the same energy, heat, and dust.

Beyond the physical cosmos, however, beyond even the intellect, we all know we're the same spirit, all of us, every soul on the planet now, and every soul that ever was or will be. We are beyond even the big bang—we are That which caused the bang. We are of the same source. This divine mystery is within all beings and all things.

Spirit-connected managers and leaders know also that unity within the company provides an edge other companies don't possess. A deeply held concept of team and a strong sense of community pull the organization toward this competitive edge.

Leaders relate to their organizations not only as mechanical systems—that is, as machines that have to be driven or "operated"—but also as communities. They take responsibility for the creation of a feeling of oneness and commonweal. They do this through strengthening and using the organization culture. They recognize organizational heroes and promulgate stories that convey the real values—hard work, customer service, and so on—of the company community. They encourage, partake in, and invent new rituals and ceremonies that bring people together (annual retreats, special staff meetings, deep sensing, and such). They openly live the organizational mythos and thus foster it.

EQUANIMITY (INNER PEACE): LEADER AS YOGI

> *Contentment is the highest form of happiness.*
>
> —Sathya Sai Baba

As a leader, your state of mind is more important than your well-knit strategies and perfectly laid plans. Robert, the general manager (chapter 1), said that his state of mind was his most important tool. It's important to manage this tool—state of mind—your own and your organization's. It's a difficult and important assignment. That's why leaders have to call on the yogi in them, for it is the yogi's traditional task to manage state of mind.

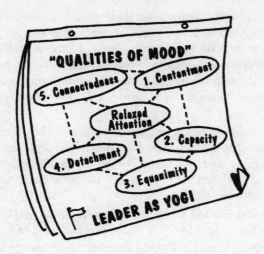

"State" refers to a loosely crocheted collection of highly interdependent and overlapping qualities of mood, such as equanimity and contentment. Here we briefly touch on five of the mood ingredients included in "state," as shown above.

1. *Contentment* is a general ease with things and life. Calmness, peace, and satisfaction are a part of it. There's a high form of happiness in contentment. It's the pure experience of happiness, not the feverishly sought "I-must-be-happy" addiction.

2. *Capacity,* we've learned, contributes an overall mood of grand welcome, an embracing. It's an intense attitude of acceptance, of allowing, of letting in. It's opening the door for higher powers to enter.

3. *Equanimity* itself is one of the most important spiritual disciplines, carrying a great cosmic secret. Self-possession is the root of it—knowing and being in control of self and senses, being composed and calm.

It's a depth of composure that's foreign to most Western thought. The Sanskrit phrase *Sama-dama-sukha* (roughly, same-minded, suffering, and happiness) helps define it. It alludes to an unaffectedness, a steadiness in the face of any circumstance whether "good" or "bad." It's a super fortitude, an equal-mindedness so unfaltering that it results in feelings of deep happiness. The great secret in this is that at some ultimate level there is really neither good nor bad. It's a matter of how we react—and our reactions depend on our steadiness of mind. We create the opposite of a vicious circle: a *victorious* circle.

Why is equanimity so important for leaders? It's the qualities of poise, perspective, peace of mind, and patience that come with it. These aren't just nice traits, they're the basic components of happiness. This, after all, is *It.* This is the peace so sought by everyone; this is the ultimate aim of it all. The spiritual discipline in equanimity is an important quality for the (spiritual) leader to cultivate. As someone said, "The reward of patience is patience."

4. *Detachment,* we've learned, grants rescue from the inevitable pain that comes with wanting. Detachment allows us to stand aside, to witness; being in the game and yet uncaught by it, being above the game, unaffected, closer to higher consciousness. Detachment is another of the spiritual cornerstones.

5. *Connectedness* refers to alertness, concentration, and focused attention even while being detached. This is the power of will, of intentionality. There's a fierceness in it. This mood supplies much energy to "state."

All of the above are fishnetted together, giving you *relaxed attention.* These "mood qualities" are states themselves and, at the same time, are qualities of and products of state. They both cause state and are causes of it. They contribute to this overall mood, and grow from it. To be in this frame of mind *is* to be any or all of them—contented, connected, detached, and so forth—knotted together. When you rise high enough into any of these moods, it's as though you pass into a cosmic black hole and get spun around, emerging more powerful, as State. It's the state of *relaxed attention.* This is the leader as yogi; this is the way of the spiritual leader.

You achieve and retain this state by being quiet and putting your attention on it—and by believing in it. You *know* with absolute assurance that deep inside you really are already-there. Relaxed attention is your already-true inner state. Calling for it isn't a matter of creating it, it's a matter of recalling it. It's connecting with higher self again.

▷ GRATITUDE (BASIC BELIEF): LEADER AS OPTIMIST

We read above that (good) management includes the evaluation and correction of performance, whereas leadership is more the acknowledgment of contributions. There's a related problem here: an error-system mentality.

What happens is that hardworking, hard-pressed management establishes "red-flag" mechanisms to detect problems so management can immediately jump on them to resolve them. The organization gradually, inadvertently becomes a problem-fixated system. The organization's basic metaphor, its primary mode of operating, and thus its central organizing principles become problem detection and resolution (or aversion). That's when the organization is in trouble (which, ironically, it doesn't see because it's too busy struggling with problems). It's living a negative focus. A "prevent" aura has taken over. Everybody is engaged in anticipating, tackling, and correcting problems. Attention is directed exclusively toward the system's problems—toward the paltry percentage of negatives in the system, rather than toward the high percentage of positives.

And management unthinkingly becomes an instrument of this negativity. You hear the word *no* more and more often in these firms, usually echoing from above. New ways of doing things are treated as threats because they may bring problems. This dampens creativity. Enthusiasm and ideas dry up. The parched pall of lethargy settles over the place. People walk around hunched over, watching their step, averting missteps. Spirit tiptoes off somewhere.

Interestingly, the number of problems in these companies doesn't diminish but expands. Why? Because they (management) become so good at it! As they are such experts at identifying and resolving problems, it's not surprising that they become just as good at creating them. That upon which we put our attention, remember, grows stronger—and this pertains to good or bad.

Management finds itself paddling upstream against a swollen river of problems. Problems, problems—until there's scant energy for anything else. Life itself becomes a problem in these companies. Organizational vitality has tiptoed away with Spirit. This condition is not an uncommon one.

Real leadership brings an opposite energy. There's lightness in it, which stems from gratitude and optimism. The leader's task is the creation of nothing less than a collective version of "right thinking" (chapter 9). This is again bringing a form of energy to the company.

The positiveness shows up as the acknowledgment of the contributions of others, rather than dwelling on errors. That's why leadership contains a large measure of back patting and award presenting; there's a grand gratefulness in it, a general aura of positiveness. It's a ball, not a pall.

Gratitude at this level is one of the most shining faces of love. It's a sky-high appreciation that includes many spiritual insights. Whole volumes, even whole lifetimes, have been devoted to seeing into the immense power of gratitude.

> Recall the bank chairman (chapter 14) who drew strength from the words, "I owe!" It is his good fortune to feel gratitude for all that has come to him in this life. He draws power from that feeling of gratitude, and that power is part of his success. He too is caught in one of those "victorious circles" mentioned earlier, and it's of his own making.
>
> He doesn't know it, and he might be embarrassed if he heard it, but that's a spiritual posture. Why? Because genuine appreciation—real gratitude—implies thankfulness to a force beyond one's worldly self, to Spirit. When he invokes gratitude, he thus lifts above the pull of the four P-words mentioned earlier (chapter 14)—pomp, power, property, and pedigree—and enriches his life.

This is none other than what the ancients in India call *sat-chit-ananda* (being-awareness-bliss), the ultimate sought-after grail of the Eastern world. Far, far above thanks and back pats, it's a valuing of existence itself, an awareness of being alive, and an appreciation of one's vitality. There's basic happiness and intense satisfaction in it. It's a reflection of inner completeness. This is the wholeness in profound integrity.

And it's up to the leader to draw this glow to the organization. This is the leader as optimist. It is this level of optimism that stamps the organization with a "can-do" spirit, an aura of grand confidence. It is this optimism that calls forth great capacity for action, for boldly stepping out when others hesitate. All true leaders are optimists. No exceptions. Optimism is power. True leaders know this.

⌐⊐ DHARMA: LEADER AS MORAL ARCHITECT
⌐⊐ VIRTUE: LEADER AS VALUES STEWARD

> *Leadership ultimately becomes*
> *moral in that it raises the level of*
> *human conduct . . . of both leader*
> *and led, and thus transforms both.*
> —James McGregor Burns

These two roles—moral architect and values steward—are, of course, the central dharma theme of the book; hence, they've been much discussed already. Here we'll simply say in summary that the main task of the leader with character is to make integrity workable in a human system. An environment saturated with integrity soaks those who inhabit it in integrity. Coming to an organization already awash in it clearly makes personal integrity easier. Good leadership creates the conditions in which people are always keeping good company. This is the leader's job.

⌐⊐ INNER/HIGHER POWER: LEADER AS WARRIOR

> *The world is full of people who*
> *have stopped thinking for*
> *themselves.*
> —Joseph Campbell

Lastly, there's a clenched-fist hardness in leadership that's seldom encountered in leadership literature. It has to do with self-reliance and personal conviction.

Conviction, in this context, means deep knowing and certainty. The word *deep* is apt because conviction is a pit-of-the-stomach phenomenon. It's the gut-level certainty good leaders possess, a sureness far beyond the level of facts or proof. It's a truth felt inside that's rock hard. There's serious self-assuredness in it.

Researchers have found that the socialization process in organizations doesn't quite take with leaders. Leaders go along with it far enough to make the allies they need, but not so far as to lose their individuality. They intuit what it takes to retain power and live their own lives in the face of the pressures of the system to knuckle under. They know that even healthy organizations—ones that foster individuality rather than damage it—still influence people and shape their behavior. Good leaders, however, are able to rise above these influences to point the way.

As a leader, you have to be your own person—to have lived your own life to the extent that you can show others the way. You have to be able to go it mostly on your own inner signals—and support others doing the same—rather than be engulfed by the club, clique, caste, or company. That's a key element in leadership: being able to hold out against society's tendency to eat you up. It's being ever ready to go beyond, or sometimes against, if necessary.

Leaders recognize this stalwartness in leadership. It shows in strong bodily signals: mostly from the gut and hands (the clenched fists, which are our ancient instruments of action). It's the *warrior* making himself known.

This is the inner warrior, the dharmic warrior, not the destructive battler the word sometimes conjures. This is the warrior that Joseph Campbell, Carlos Castaneda, Will Stillwell, Carol Pearson, Robert Bly, and others have written of. This is the warrior as personal power, as staunch hero, the inner loner, the person of action; the warrior as free spirit in the true, untethered sense of the term, both free and Spirit.

Because there's energy and primitiveness in the warrior, society (whether it's the company society or the larger society) loves to surround it and neutralize these "dangerous" qualities. But the true warrior doesn't allow society's fetters. The true warrior doesn't hesitate to act when inner truth impels action—even when there's pressure not to act. As he or she is in constant spiritual awareness, the warrior maintains an attitude of unbending intent.

CHAPTER 18

A VISIT WITH A 6,000-YEAR-OLD KING

> *Leaders should lead as far as they can and then vanish. Their ashes should not choke the fire they have lit.*
>
> —H.G. Wells

There's another aspect of leadership with hardness in it that hasn't been covered well enough yet. It has to do with the variance between what leaders experience leadership to be and what the literature says it is.

To get at this, we turn to another ancient/modern story and end the book in the presence of an interesting old man and his provocative truth. We call him from the dusty, long-forgotten archives of prehistory—probably more than 6,000 years ago—to find that his words are curiously right for us today. Here's our rendition of the story:

> Wounded, lying on a bed of arrows in the center of a vibrant-hued tent is an old man. From his bearing and clothing he's obviously a king. He's breathing softly. His once-vigorous body is now weak, on the brink of death. His name is Bhishma.
>
> Bhishma is revered throughout the world for his integrity. He was even told by God that he was the greatest man who ever graced the world of men. Bhishma has lived a long life, which, like all lives, has included struggle and suffering. But

he is the epitome of dharma and has gone through it all without once going against his vow to uphold dharma. Even the loss of his rightful kingdom did not keep him from following his dharma.

Bhishma has been asked by the young king who just defeated him in battle for advice on the art of being a leader. Pleased, ready to serve, the old king stirs and begins talking. His body is frail, yet he speaks with steady, unaffected detachment.

"Some of the most intricate knots of the mysteries of the universe are bound up in leadership. I have been behind the veil of death and thus know many things, so listen to these words.

"It is not easy to rule well and a king's one worldly duty is to rule well. He is essentially a man of action, not destiny. It is action which shapes destiny, not the other way around.

"A king's highest duty is to the gods; next, of equal importance, is Truth. Truth is the highest refuge; all the world rests on Truth.

"He should be straightforward in both words and conduct.

"He should know when to conceal his own weaknesses (the weaknesses in his kingdom).

"There is a danger in mildness. The king should not be too mild or he will then be disregarded. The people will not have enough respect for him and his words. He must also avoid the other extreme, being too fierce, for then the people will be afraid of him, which is not a happy state of affairs.

"Compassion must be a part of his mental makeup, but he must guard against displaying a too-forgiving nature, for then he will be considered weak by low men and will be taken advantage of.

"Alertness is greatly necessary. He must study his foes and friends incessantly.

"His first duty is to his people. He should take care of them with no thoughts of pleasing himself, subordinating his own wishes and desires to those of the people. He should guard them as a mother guards the child.

"The king needs to be careful not to place implicit confidence in anyone. He should keep his innermost thoughts concealed from even his nearest and dearest.

"You need to know when to seek protection in your fort when your position is weak. And you should be ready to make peace with a foe who is stronger.

"Be pleasant in speech.

"Surround yourself with people of like nature, who have qualities that are noble. The only difference between you and your officers is the white umbrella signifying your higher office.

"The people should live in freedom and happiness, as they do in their father's house. The very essence of your role is to protect the people and their happiness. It is not easy to secure people's happiness. You need to use diverse methods. Skill, cleverness, and truth, all three are important.

"Pay attention to the state of the kingdom. Old and ramshackle surroundings are symbols of disregard. Renovate, to win good opinion.

"Know how to use the powers of punishment and do not hesitate to use them on miscreants. People are often led by chastisement. Know, then, the science of chastisement.

"Self-interest is the most powerful factor in the life of everyone. No one is dear to another unless there is some gain involved.

"The treasury should always be full.

"Supervise the work of all your officers yourself.

"Never trust the guardians of the city or fort implicitly.

"Do things in secret from your enemies. You can never protect the kingdom by candor and by simplicity. You should be both candid and crooked.

"A king who is honored by his subjects will naturally be

respected by his foes, and will be feared by them also.

"Nothing, not even the smallest act, can be accomplished by a single man. He has to have assistance.

"Never confide plans that are in danger of being disapproved to righteous people, even those who are firmly determined to serve your side.

"The king can't be too careful. Wicked people may appear honest; honest ones may appear dishonest. The honest person is likely to become dishonest, for no one can always be of the same mind.

"No one should be trusted completely. And yet, a want of trust is also wrong. The policy: mistrust as well as trust.

"Harbor no malice, absolutely none, in your heart.

"Dharma [integrity, right action, morality] is the watchword of a king. *Nothing* is more powerful! To the extent you yield or diminish dharma, to that degree disintegrity sets in.

"Death is nearing every creature every moment. What you have planned to do tomorrow must be done today, forenoon! Death is ruthless. It will never wait and see if all your projects are carried out. Readiness for it is important. The world is but a passing pageant.

"Man is born alone and he dies alone. He has not a single companion on his march through this incident called life. The spouse, the father, the mother, sons, kinsmen, friends, all turn away from your body and go about their work. Only dharma follows the body. That is the only friend of man, and the only thing he should seek."

With that, Bhishma smiles slightly and pauses to signal he has finished.

People become quiet when they read this story. They have to sit for a while and contemplate what this old man is revealing. It's a pensive, subdued silence. They expected sage advice from a wise king and now aren't sure what they've gotten. Within the quietness, however, is a sure echo of truth and the feeling there's something of value here.

For one thing, Bhishma bumps us up against the truth that this is an imperfect world, and that the game of leadership is played in this world. He reminds us that the worldly game is ultimately about winning (which may not mean defeating someone). His message: win. Be true to yourself.

He's also saying we need a toughness to match the roughness of the world. And he's telling us that in this world we must take care of ourselves, our people, *and* take care of business.

Bhishma grounds us so firmly in the world that he helps us rise above it. He cares not a jot for consistency and plays this worldly game with unblinking, unapologetic straightness. There's always something in truth, no matter how hard it is, that raises us up.

His presence, there on his bed of arrows, bequeaths the final truth that in the end we've got to be our own person, alone. That's all we've got. It's the profound reality that *the* truth is inside rather than in theories and concepts that come from outside. This, after all, is dharma; this is the ultimate spirituality.

APPENDIX

A GLIMPSE INTO THE
SATHYA SAI BABA PHENOMENON

> *Remember Dharma, practice Dharma.*
>
> —Sathya Sai Baba

Here, for the interested or curious, we glance at the remarkable holy man Sai Baba—who he is, what he does, what his miracles mean, and the universality of his teachings, many of which have inspired this book.

As I prepare to write this, I hear his voice, there's a smile in it, "Why do you make me the appendix when you know I am the heart?" I know he already knows the answer, but I go along with his word play. "Not a bodily appendix, Swami, a book appendix. So people have choice. If this information were in the main part of the book, readers would feel obligated to read it, and some may not be that interested, and others may think it sounds 'religious.' My original contract was for a nonreligious book on spirituality in management."

"Good," says the voice.

THE WORLDLY SAI

To his followers, Sai Baba is a divine incarnation, an avatar, a god-man. Notwithstanding these seemingly otherworldly origins, there is some in-the-world information about him.

Sathya Sai Baba (literally, "Truth, Mother-Father") took birth in 1926 in a hot, dusty little hamlet on the banks of a river in southern India. There wasn't even a road to it. He is the second of three incarnations of Sai Baba.

The first Sai Baba was a unique Indian holy man born in 1835. After some initial wandering, he spent all his days at Shirdi, a small town northeast of Bombay. He was much revered for teaching the unity of man and God and had a great following among Hindus and Muslims, who both claimed him as their own. People who know India appreciate how rare this is.

The present avatar, Sathya Sai Baba, will leave his body at age ninety-six in the year 2022. The third Sai Baba called Prema Sai (Sanskrit for "Love") will be born shortly thereafter. A series of sacred incarnations such as this is very uncommon in India.

The compiler of Baba's *Discourses on the Bhagavad Gita* (Drucker 1988, 262-63) wrote of the public Sai Baba:

> Now, a modern township has sprung up called Prasanthi Nilayam [Abode of Peace], which encloses Sai Baba's ashram and which houses a comprehensive educational complex that has students from all parts of India and abroad living and studying together in a primary school, and then going on to the high school, and on to the college and university levels, and then on to the post-graduate and doctoral levels. The Sri Sathya Sai educational system, with [29] campuses in various states of India, is wholly nondenominational and cost-free. Also at Prasanthi Nilayam is the central headquarters for the worldwide network of thousands of Sri Sathya Sai organizations, engaged in a wide range of community service projects and in bringing education in human values into school systems throughout the world.
>
> [Also being completed there is a new airport capable of handling commercial jets. This airport will offer scheduled and chartered air service for the throngs of visitors pouring into this rural area. In addition, there is the recently com-

pleted Institute of Higher Medical Sciences, a high-tech hospital offering the latest in medical care technology—open heart surgery and organ transplants, also cost-free.]

The hub of all this activity is Sri Sathya Sai Baba, who from his earliest days has attracted large numbers of people to him through his unique personal presence. He can only be described as pure, selfless love personified, the embodiment of perfect peace and bliss, the essence of all goodness. He manifests every noble human quality that mankind admires, and he incorporates every divine quality that is characteristic of an Avatar. He has the full power of nature in his hand. He has all knowledge at his command. He knows the past, present, and future of everyone who comes to him.

In his teachings, he harbors all faiths and emphasizes the unity of all religious experience and the oneness of divinity. In his personal manner and expression, Baba displays a majestic grace, and at the same time, an exquisite joyfulness. In the midst of the splendor that surrounds him, he lives a simple, austere life, completely committed to the service of those to whom he ministers. Not being limited to the physical plane, he works in all dimensions, appearing through visions and dreams and inner experiences. Guiding spiritual unfoldment he inspires from within and directs from without. He illuminates the heart and transforms the mind and reveals the greatest of all treasures . . . Atma [the Divinity that resides in each of us].

At various workshops and conferences, people have asked Louise and me to talk about Sai Baba. After we provide brief preliminary information about him, we begin answering questions and concerns regarding Sai Baba. Here's a loose composite of questions we've heard over the years:

> Who is Sai Baba? Where is he? What's he do? What's his mission, his purpose?
>
> Why do you go there? What do you do there?
>
> What will I get from it if I go?
>
> Will I be able to see and talk to him?

Does he really do "miracles"? Is he a magician? Have you seen him do them? Are they real?

Does he charge anything?

What if you don't believe, if you're skeptical?

In what ways has going there changed you? What have you learned?

Will I lose "me" there? Is it a cult? Will he kidnap me? [accompanied with laughter]

Why does he wear his hair that way?

Is he very old-fashioned? Is he nonfeminist?

Is he really as loving as they say? Does everyone feel it?

Could going there (or even reading about it) be a "sin"—you know, false Gods and such?

Are there any books about him I could read?

Trying to respond to such a broad range of issues one by one doesn't work very well. It sounds logical, but it often misses the point. Better to use some other people's writings and tell some stories (we know that people can learn what they need to learn from stories).

PERSPECTIVES

Roger is an American businessman. He has a PhD in one of the social sciences. It's his first visit to Sai Baba's ashram and his first time in India. He heard of Baba several years ago and, after avoiding the trip, has finally come. Here are some excerpts from a letter to his daughter.

I felt perhaps I'd been called, and felt, quite seriously, that if I missed the chance, it might be the same as being told Christ had come and I had a chance to sit at his feet, but had other, better things to do.

My uncertainties vanished when I stepped off the plane at Bombay. I felt a sense of peace, an inner knowing that I was on the right path, that this trip was right, and I'd be okay. That

*feeling of "rightness" persisted even when the taxi driver mistook
my English, and delivered me first to some fleabag hotel, and it
continued when I finally arrived the next evening at the ashram
when it was late, and there was no one to help with my luggage,
and the door of the building where I was to stay was padlocked.
Even after I got in, one of my erstwhile roommates told me to get
lost, it's too late, that I should come back in the morning.
(Funnily enough, that was the last cross word I heard—this is a
peaceful place!) My equanimity outlasted these experiences as it
never would have at home!*

*The second morning I was here, I began the practice I've fol-
lowed since, of getting up at 4 A.M. and going to the temple for
the daybreak ceremonies, which consist of chanting Om twenty-
one times. It was pouring down rain, a perfect torrential tropical
storm, when I ventured out in the pitch black that morning. I
almost didn't go, but something impelled me to wade through
the ankle-deep water rushing through the streets. Once seated in
the temple, I was saturated with the most intense feeling of love
I've ever experienced. It was not a feeling either of loving or
being loved, but of being love, of existing as love and in love . . .
so sweet and so wonderful that I couldn't stop sobbing with joy.
That feeling has not come again so strongly, either in the temple
or outside; but it was my sign, my talisman, my welcoming, and
it buoys me up during the down, discouraging periods which are
inevitable in this or any kind of inner work.*

*The feeling hereabouts is that Sai Baba is more than a saint or
guru, that He is an avatar, God incarnate, like Jesus, Krishna,
or the Buddha. That's easier to believe than to disbelieve here.*

Just before Roger leaves to return to America, we're sitting in
the canteen. I comment on how quickly and sensitively he
has picked up on all this—even the subtler things. He sits
quietly a moment, looks at me, and says, "I'm almost sixty,
Jack. I can't waste time if I am to come home before dark."

This is also Van's first visit to the ashram. He's a physician
and president-director of a private medical group in the
States. He has been attending a medical conference in Banga-

lore and side-tripped here. After a week or so he is called in for a group "interview" with Baba.

I see him two days later. "Congratulations," I say, "when Baba called you, you looked like a wide receiver who had just caught the winning touchdown." He laughs and tells me what happened.

"I was sitting in the inner room," he says, "watching Baba materialize two rings and a pendant out of thin air for some people. Just—pop!—and there they were. I was astounded. As I sat there thinking how nice it would be to take something back to my staff, Baba turned to me as if he were listening to my thoughts. 'What do you want, sir?' he asked. Astonished, I stammered, 'Uh . . . something for the staff.'

"Then Baba swished his hand around in the air a couple of times and a glass egglike thing, which I've since learned is a lingam, appeared in his fingers and he handed it to me!" Van reaches into his pocket and pulls out the two-inch ovate object. It's white with a marbleized brown in it.

He holds it up, squints closely at it a few moments as though to reconfirm something to himself, and then holds it out for me to examine. "It's changing shape!" he almost whispers, great wonder in his voice. "I've been watching it. See, there's a small ridge forming there . . . and there!" We're standing in the street, two virtual strangers with our heads close together trying to scrutinize the object from the same angle. His eyes drift away, perplexed, his forehead furrows, he's deep in thought. This little gift for his staff is obviously unseating beliefs set in place by a lifetime in the hard sciences. After a moment Van looks at me, relieved, as though he just found his way out of a dilemma. "It's a new physics," he says.

I've heard hundreds of stories of these materialized presents and have seen scores of them myself, and so the sharp edges of my doubt have smoothed a little over the years. But this particular lingam lingers in my thoughts. It's the changing shape that's special. It's not only an extraordinary physical happening, there's also a wondrous inner significance to it.

Everyone who comes to Sai Baba may not receive a lingam, but we all get a priceless gift here. It's a boon far beyond the material; it's the gift of unconditional, growing love. Some come here from curiosity, others out of despair. Some come only to see the so-called miracles. But love is the unexpected gift for all who come—even the doubters, even the skeptics. Each of us comes with a different capacity for receiving love (and thus loving), and the gift of love we receive here perfectly matches our individual readiness. And now it becomes clearer that from the moment we receive it, the love constantly reshapes, expanding to keep pace with our ever-growing capacity to receive.

> A few months ago while waiting for Sai Baba to come out for morning *darshan,* I strike up a quiet conversation with an Indian man sitting next to me. He's from Calcutta and has visited this ashram several times. He has also visited many other spiritual places throughout India.
>
> I explain this book in progress and ask him, as a pilgrim, for his perspective on all this. He's quiet for several moments. I assume the question was unclear and begin to rephrase it, when he interrupts. "I understand your question. It's a good one. I want to answer it carefully."
>
> A few moments later he looks at me and says, "This place is unique. The emphasis here, rightly, is on service to mankind. There is only one other pilgrimage place in India that does that: Ramakrishnamath. And here, there's also a constant emphasis on one's spiritual development." He shakes his head, "It's very, very strong here. In other places they often focus on rituals."

UNIVERSAL TEACHER

> *Not a religion, but the spirit behind all religions.*
> —Juan Mascaro
> (referring to *The Upanishads*)

In the introduction we read that there's a difference between religion and spirituality. It's important to keep that distinction in mind when trying to figure Sai Baba. He's a universal teacher, which means his spiritual message transcends the boundaries of particular religions.

Baba speaks of his universality:

"Rain falling in different parts of the world flows through thousands of channels to reach the ocean . . . and so, too, religions and theologies, which all come from man's yearning for meaning; they, too, flow in a thousand ways, fertilizing many fields, refreshing tired people, and at last reach the Ocean."

Baba's mission is to help everyone who comes to him reach the ocean, whatever their background. Visitors to the ashram find that he actively encourages them to practice their own religion.

In another context Baba says:

"The universe around you is a pleasant garden-bed, full of charming patches of many-hued flowers filled with fragrance and nectarine elixir—each bed being a religion attracting the loyalty of millions of sincere seekers."

Continue your worship along the lines already familiar to you . . . . There is no need to change your chosen God and adopt a new one after you have seen and heard Me.
—Sathya Sai Baba

Another quote from Roger's letter to his daughter:

Sai Baba himself lives very simply in one small room, taking very little food, wearing identical, one-piece, orange cotton robes each day, and devoting all his time to the service of his flock. He is not particularly humble . . . but he obviously cares nothing for material things for himself.

He says he is not here to found a new cult or religion, and indeed symbols of all the world's great religions are displayed prominently in and on the temple and elsewhere. He encourages people to practice whatever religion they're comfortable with. His mission, he says, is to help each of us to come home . . . and to live up to our divinity.

Here I have glimpsed a way of living which, while challenging in the extreme, is richly rewarding . . . based on love, on service, on giving up material striving, and on forbearance and nonviolence in words and deeds, and peacefulness toward all.

MIRACLES

> *Miracles happen, not in opposition to nature, but in opposition to what we know of nature.*
>
> —Saint Augustine

Many people first hear of Baba in connection with his many "miracles." Some skeptics pooh-pooh the miracles as just magic tricks; others consider them only as *siddhis* (the ability to perform feats that defy natural law), which are quite common in India.

There's no commonsense explanation for such "beyond nature" happenings. Spiritual people call them "miracles." To certain artistic people these happenings are "manifestations." Some visionaries see them as previews of the capabilities of humanity as it will super-evolve in the future. Certain scientists consider them "paranormal" or "psychic phenomena"; others simply ignore these happenings because the facts don't fit into any known stall or pigeonhole. To the devotees of Sai Baba they are convincing symbols of his love. To Baba himself they're simply his nature.

People who have been around Sai Baba for a long time, who have witnessed hundreds of these "miracles" also tend to downplay them, but for a vastly different reason than the skeptics'. They are personally experiencing the even more unbelievable miracle of transformation that is taking place within themselves—and they are seeing and feeling and hearing of the countless, deep personal transformations occurring within the throngs of people at the ashram and around the world.

Many come to observe his miracles and stay on to experience the great personal growth that accrues to those who come to this place. The miracles force an expansion of consciousness: it's like opening the gates in our scientific stalls and being invited to gallop out beyond our limits. We're reminded that we need to shift our beliefs, that there's more to this life than we think we know.

We're pulled by a greater force than we can imagine beyond our knowledge, beyond our doubts, beyond our cognitive boundaries, closer and closer to real wisdom. The miraculous (paranormal) events fly in the face of our scientific rationalism and nudge (or blast) us beyond.

"See for yourself" is Baba's typically simple recipe for making all of this less complicated.

Drawing by Nina O'Connell

THE LARGER MIRACLE: LOVE

As profound as that expansion of awareness may be, there's even more to it than that. It's the love here.

Lawrence Babb (1986), an anthropologist (not a Sai devotee), came to India to study this holy man—not only the miracles but the whole phenomenon. I excerpt and paraphrase some of his observations:

Sai Baba's magic and his persona are unintelligible unless seen against the background of his lovingness and his play (his *leelas*, as the play is called). Playfulness, it must never be forgotten, is a close sibling of love. Real love, like play, is utterly spontaneous, free, uncalculating, and its own justification. The devotees enter into a playful love affair with him.

There is sheer magicality in his miracles, yes, but the real miracle is not mere magic. (To India, magic hardly carries much weight.) It is what it signifies. They're his *leelas*, his sports. They're not *siddhis*, they're spontaneous, Godlike play . . . evidence of his "otherness," of his favor; expressions of joyousness shared with the playmate-devotees. [In other words, they're manifestations not of trinkets but of love— and, they're potentially available to all.]

Belief in him is not just the belief that he possesses extraordinary powers; it's the belief that his powers have extraordinary implications. The sense of Baba's abounding love [and] this feeling of being personally loved by Baba despite the large crowds there . . . is the root source of the spiritual energy of his presence. [His love is his power.]

There's much more to him than meets the eye. He's no mere magician, but a teacher and moralist. His divine character invests the widest field of human experience with a kind of unified moral sense. His recipe: not how to lead a virtuous life [but] how to lead a life in which virtue has meaning.

As playmate-parent, he mainly teaches trust in him, which is trust in existence. In the West it's akin, perhaps, to Erik Erikson's "basic trust," which basically is that "somebody is there." It's a primordial confidence . . . there [with Baba], you are "someone" with a place in a meaningful and just cosmos. Whatever the vicissitudes of life, it looks different in the perspective of a personal relationship with Baba.

There's really nothing very subtle about this; the central ingredient is people's confidence in his love for them . . . and their own feelings of love for him in return. It is not logic but love that finally cements this system

Everyone who has contact with Sai Baba, whether by physically going to India or by going within—wherever in the world that person may be—and meditating on him, feels singled out for his special love.

PEACE

There's something else magical about the ashram: peace. It comes with the love and trust, and comes from being connected with Spirit rather than attached to the material matters in the outside world.

> My Telugu friend plopped down next to me one day. We grunted "Hello" in unison. I had been quite busy and thus we hadn't seen each other for quite a while. He probably thought I was too tied up in work. We sat quietly for several minutes. Finally, he laughed, a little shyly, preparing to say something, but then, unaccustomed to offering advice, changed his mind and became silent again. A moment or two later, looking the other way, he spoke as if to himself, but loudly enough so I could hear, "Ah, our time in this life is so short, and it is eaten up by worry and work."

> _____

> Later, another Indian, from his attire a poor man from some nearby village, sits next to me. In this part of the world a foreigner is something rare and interesting, and the locals don't bother hiding their curiosity. He sat, blank-faced, staring at me, eyeing me up and down—my garb, the books I carried, my white skin (burning in the hot sun). Assuming he didn't speak any English and thinking his attention would go elsewhere when his interest ebbed, I just sat there, semiaware of his scrutiny.

> After a while, with the same stone countenance, he leaned over and in the proper, lilting English of educated Indians said, "You find peace of mind here. That's good."

Andrew has been on the spiritual path for a long time, mostly in the States and Europe. He tells of his first visit to India to see Sai Baba. His smile is so broad it makes slits of his eyes as he talks.

> "I'm in the little marriage hall in Whitefield. I look around. It's a simple, undecorated, white-walled room with some twirling fans in the ceiling. Everyone is sitting on the floor, quietly waiting for Baba.

> "Then, people stir a little, stretching to look toward the door at the side. And in walks this little brown man with bushy

hair wearing an orange robe. Nobody announces him, no fanfare, nothing. He just slowly walks in, looks out lovingly at the crowd, blesses them with a wave of his hand, glides over, and sits down.

"I'm used to special lights, TV cameras and monitors along the walls, fancy flowers, music, a mammoth picture of the guru on the stage, and all that. And here I am in this place, with this person who reportedly doesn't even accept any money, and he walks over and sits in an ordinary office chair! And I knew I was home. Years of searching, long periods of despondency and depression; and now, suddenly, I'm very happy!"

When people come to see Baba, concerns about cult seem to evaporate. Baba often doesn't let you hang around too long. He relentlessly demands that people *not* become attached to his bodily form. "You've been here too long," he says. "Leave. Stop meditating. Go home and serve others. Put these principles into practice." He's sweet about it, but emphatic.

Here are some quotes from Dr. Sam Sandweiss's second book (1985, 149-50) about his experiences with Sai Baba. Sam's quotes include some of Baba's words:

Thoughts of my recent stay at Prasanthi Nilayam came, bringing great peace. Sitting eight to ten hours a day in quiet meditation in his divine presence had left me feeling cleansed and with new insight. The heaviness of my active, hectic life in America seemed washed away.

Gone was the impulse to overeat, overwork, or become lost in meaningless television. Stripped for the moment of attachment to family and profession, of desire for luxury and materialism, I awakened to a feeling which seemed somehow familiar, yet never before experienced in this lifetime. My inner [higher] life had become so peaceful and unruffled it seemed more attractive than the outerworld. I felt content in just being still; there was no need to struggle. I could stay here forever.

Baba had granted me a brief glimpse into a profound inner truth: *exquisite peace really does exist within*. [Emphasis mine.]

[Sam quotes Baba]:

> *People seek joy and contentment from external objects, though there are treasures inside themselves. They arise from the Lord who is inherent in them, everywhere. Underground we have a stream of potable water; between us and the stream there is a thick bed of soil. By spiritual work that soil has to be removed. So too, peace and contentment exist deep within the conscious-ness of everyone, but they are overlaid by thick beds of . . . tendencies and habits (greed, hatred, lust, desire, pride, jealousy, attachment to the outer world) and so, man has to remove these in order to benefit from the treasure.*

[Sam again]:

> I knew I would go back to my home, no question about that. I loved my family and they needed me; I had duties to perform, obligations to fulfill. But in this moment of reflec-tion, I saw more deeply into Baba's mystery . . . from my limited consciousness I had begun to see the inner life as more attractive than the outer . . .

[Sam quoting Baba again]:

> *Life is a song—sing it.*
> *Life is a game—play it.*
> *Life is a challenge—meet it.*
> *Life is a dream—realize it.*
> *Life is a sacrifice—offer it.*
> *Life is love—enjoy it.*

[Sam continues]:

> Now, in this peaceful moment, I could feel so clearly that the purpose of life, when one is made empty and without desire, is to love the Lord and to express that love in kindness to others.

WHAT IS HE?

Louise and I are back in California, in a shopping mall. We run into some old friends, a couple we haven't talked with in over two years. We sit down for a cup of espresso. Their questions come: "How long have you been away? Where have you been? Huh! To India? At an ashram? Um, what did you learn there?" They seem genuinely interested, so we try to explain by talking about many of the things in this book: believing, loving, detachment, awareness of spirit—those kinds of things. But it's hard to convey in that busy atmosphere, even with old friends.

After quite a bit more talk, it comes out. I say, "Going to Sai Baba often entails a sort of total rethink of the concept of God." "Oh, is that all?" he laughs, his quick humor underscoring the depth of what we're talking about.

His wife leans forward. "What does that mean?" she asks, referring to my comment about rethinking the concept of God. I continue, "God is, well, dispersed energy, formless. God isn't a person or object in this world. And that formless energy is closer, more real than we think; it's a part of you, and you're a part of it." The conversation continues around that subject for a while; it's earnest and interesting but it never quite clicks. It's hard, especially for us Westerners, to grasp a beyond-theology God.

A few weeks later we're back in India. I'm meditating. In my mind-wandering reveries, I see Louise and me back in the Sistine Chapel in the Vatican. It's twenty years after our first visit. A lot of time and life has gone by since then, since the Catholic boy stood there craning his neck wondrously at Michelangelo's masterpiece painting far, oh so far, far above on the ceiling.

In the painted sky is God: a huge, fierce, bearded figure with lightning flashing from the clouds behind him. And there is man, below god, lying on his back, propped on one elbow, naked, reaching up, up, upward for God—their fingers almost, but not quite, touching; straining, stretching, but not quite meeting. The beauty of the work, the tension in that little gap is awesome!

As I recall that scene, we are again in the Chapel. Twenty years older, different physically, mentally, and spiritually. Our necks, a little stiffer nowadays, are again tilted ninety degrees upward, trying to take in the magnificence of the fresco.

As I squint, I notice that the ceiling begins to shimmer, as though transforming into vibrations of color and shape. I catch my breath! Smoothly, noiselessly the magnificent chapel roof clamshells open and disappears.

It's midafternoon. I expect the Roman sun to come streaming upon us, but it doesn't. That's not sky up there, it's light—a very bright but soft luminescence.

It hovers and then seems to move toward us, slowly spreading downward—perhaps we're floating upward toward it—until we're enveloped by it. We're in the light. No more floor, no more benches along the walls, or even walls—no sense of existing in a particular location, no feeling of whereness. Just light—a brilliant, soft, comfortable, friendly, enfolding radiance.

I glance toward Louise and she's not there, she has faded into the glow. I feel not a trace of alarm, knowing all is right in this light. Mildly curious, I reach to touch where she was to see if there's anything recognizable in that space. As I do, I find that my arm is not visible, and I notice that my shoulder and body aren't there. I find that I, too, have folded into the glow. And then I realize, we *are* it, for these precious moments we've been brought into that light and have become it. We're home.

For more information on Sai Baba, or for a list of the many books that have been written about this phenomenon, contact the Sathya Sai Baba Book Center of America, 305 West First Street, Tustin, CA 92680, or call (714) 669-0522.

References and Recommended Reading

Adams, J., ed. 1984. *Transforming work*. Alexandria, Va.: Miles River Press.
Adams, J., ed. 1986. *Transforming leadership*. Alexandria, Va.: Miles River Press.
Assagioli, R. 1971. *The act of will*. New York: Penguin.
Autry, J. 1991. *Love and profit*. New York: Morrow.
Babb, L. 1986. *Redemptive encounters*. Berkeley: University of California Press.
Badaracco, J. L., and R. R. Ellsworth. 1989. *Leadership and the quest for integrity*. Boston: Harvard Business School Press.
Baskin, D. 1990. *Divine memories of Sathya Sai Baba*. Tustin, Calif.: Sathya Sai Book Center.
Bass, B. 1985. *Leadership and performance beyond expectations*. New York: Free Press.
Batten, J. 1989. *Tough-minded leadership*. New York: Amacom.
Bennis, W. 1989. *On becoming a leader*. Reading, Mass.: Addison-Wesley.
Bennis, W., and B. Nanus. 1985. *Leaders: The strategies of taking charge*. New York: Harper & Row.
Benson, H. 1975. *The relaxation response*. New York: Morrow.
Benson, H. 1987a. *Beyond the relaxation response*. New York: Berkley Books.
Benson, H. 1987b. *Your maximum mind*. New York: Random House.
Blanchard, K., and S. Johnson. 1982. *The one minute manager*. New York: Morrow.
Blanchard, K., and N. V. Peale. 1988. *The power of ethical management*. New York: Morrow.
Blitz, M. 1991. Leadership course.
Block, P. 1987. *The empowered manager*. San Francisco: Jossey-Bass.
Blumberg, S. 1983. *Win-win administration*. Sun Lakes, Ariz.: Thomas Horton.
Bly, R. 1990. *Iron John*. Reading, Mass.: Addison-Wesley.
Brouwers, A. 1980. *Seeing beyond a new horizon*. Venlo, Netherlands: Uitgeverij Van Spijk.
Buhler, G., trans. 1969. *The laws of Manu*. New York: Dover.
Burns, J. 1978. *Leadership*. New York: Harper & Row.
Buscaglia, L. 1972. *Love*. New York: Fawcett.
Capra, F. 1977. *The tao of physics*. New York: Bantam Books.
Chakraborty, S. K. 1989. *Foundations of managerial work: Contributions from Indian thought*. Bombay: Himalaya Publishing House.
Chakraborty, S. K., ed. 1990. *Human response development: Exploring transformational values*. New Delhi: Wiley Eastern.
Chopra, D. 1988. *Return of the Rishi*. Boston: Houghton Mifflin.
Conger, J., and R. Kanungo. 1988. *Charismatic leadership*. San Francisco: Jossey-Bass.
Cornelssen, L. 1986. *Hunting the I*. Tiruvannamalai, India: Centenary Publications.

Cornwell, J. 1991. *The hiding places of God.* New York: Warner.

Cousins, N. 1979. *Anatomy of an illness.* New York: Bantam Books.

Covey, S. 1990. *The seven habits of highly effective people.* New York: Fireside.

Decter, J. 1989. *Nicholas Roerich: The life and art of a Russian master.* Rochester, Vt.: Park Street Press.

Deal, T., and A. Kennedy. 1982. *Corporate cultures.* Reading, Mass.: Addison-Wesley.

DePree, M. 1989. *Leadership is an art.* New York: Doubleday.

Dewey, E. 1971. *Cycles: The mysterious forces that trigger events.* New York: Hawthorne.

Dossey, L. 1992. *Meaning and medicine.* New York: Bantam Books.

Drucker, A., ed. 1988. *Bhagawan Sri Sathya Sai Baba: Discourses on the Bhagavad Gita.* N.p.

Etzioni, A. 1988. *The moral dimension: Toward a new economics.* New York: Free Press.

Ferguson, M. 1980. *The Aquarian conspiracy.* Los Angeles: Tarcher.

Fordyce, J., and R. Weil. 1979. *Managing with people.* Reading, Mass.: Addison-Wesley.

Foster, R. 1978. *Celebration of discipline: The path to spiritual growth.* New York: Harper & Row

Gardner, J. 1990. *On leadership.* New York: Free Press.

Gendlen, E. 1978. *Focusing.* New York: Everest House.

Greenleaf, R. 1977. *Servant leadership: A journey into the nature of legitimate power & greatness.* Mahweh, N.J.: Paulist Press.

Grinder, J., and R. Bandler. 1981. *Trance-formations: Neuro-Linguistic Programming and the structure of hypnosis.* Edited by C. Andreas. Moab, Utah: Real People Press.

Grof, S., ed. 1984. *Ancient wisdom and modern science.* Albany: State University of New York Press.

Grosso, M. 1992. *Frontiers of the soul.* Wheaton, Ill.: Quest Books.

Gunther, M. 1977. *The luck factor.* New York: Macmillan.

Haraldsson, E. 1987. *Miracles are my visiting cards: An investigative report on the psychic phenomena associated with Sathya Sai Baba.* London: Century.

Harman, W. 1990. *Global mind change: A new age revolution in the way we think.* New York: Warner.

Harrison, R. 1975. "Diagnosing organizational ideology." In *The 1975 handbook for group facilitators,* edited by University Associates. La Jolla, Calif.: University Associates.

Harrison, R. 1983. Strategies for a new age. *Human Resource Management* 22(3): 209–35.

Hawley, J. A. 1984. Vertical linking in organizations. *Organizational Dynamics* (Winter).

Hawley. J. S., ed. 1987. *Saints and virtues.* Berkeley:University of California Press.

Hill, R. 1983. *Hanta yo: An American saga.* New York: Warner.

Hislop, J. 1985. *My Baba and I.* San Diego: Birth Day.

Hoff, B. 1982. *The tao of Pooh.* New York: Dutton.

Iacocca, L. 1984. *Iacocca: An autobiography.* New York: Bantam Books.

Jamplonsky, G. 1983. *Teach only love.* New York: Bantam Books.

Kanter, R. 1984. *The change masters.* New York: Touchstone Books.

Keyes, K. 1974. *Handbook to higher consciousness.* Berkeley, Calif.: Living Love Center.

King, A. 1974. Expectation effects in organizational change. *Administrative Science Quarterly* (June).

Koestenbaum, P. 1991. *The heart of business*. Old Saybrook, Conn.: Saybrook.

Kotter, J. P., and J. Heslett. 1992. *Corporate culture and performance*. New York: Free Press.

Kouzes, J., and B. Pozner. 1990. *The leadership challenge*. San Francisco: Jossey-Bass.

Krystal, P. 1984. *Cutting the ties that bind*. Los Angeles: Aura Books.

Kubler-Ross, E. 1976. *On death and dying*. New York: Macmillan.

Kushner, H. 1981. *When bad things happen to good people*. New York: Avon.

Lair, J. 1985. *I ain't much, baby, but I'm all I've got*. New York: Fawcett.

LeCron, L. 1970. *Self-hypnotism*. New York: Signet.

LeShan, L. 1978. *How to meditate*. London: Sphere Books.

Levin, H. 1985. *Good chances*. Tustin, Calif.: Sathya Sai Book Center.

McCarthy, M. 1991. *Mastering the information age*. Los Angeles: Tarcher.

McGuire, B. 1974. Safety F.I.R.S.T. *Fire Command* (April).

Mascaro, J., trans. 1965. *The Upanishads*. London: Penguin.

Mascaro, J., trans. 1971. *The Bhagavad Gita*. London: Penguin.

Matsushita, K. 1984. *Not for bread alone: A business ethos, a management ethic*. Tokyo: PHP Institute.

Morrisey, G. 1992. *Creating your future*. San Francisco: Berrett-Koehler.

Murphet, H. 1971. *Sai Baba, man of miracles*. London: Frederick Miller.

Murphet, H. 1977. *Sai Baba avatar*. San Diego: Birth Day.

Musashi, M. 1982. *The book of five rings* (Gorin no sho). New York: Bantam Books.

Naisbitt, J. 1982. *Megatrends*. New York: Warner.

Narasimhan, V. K. 1985. *From Bapu to Baba*. Madras, India: Kalakshetra.

Nisargadatta, M. 1973. *I am that*. Durham, N.C.: Acorn.

Nystrom, P., and W. Starbuck. 1984. To avoid organizational crises, unlearn. *Organizational Dynamics* (Spring).

Oliver, M. 1990. Removing the veils. *Sanathana Sarathi* (December).

O'Toole, J. 1985. *Vanguard management*. New York: Doubleday.

Ouchi, W. 1980. *Theory z*. Reading, Mass.: Addison-Wesley.

Owen, H. 1984. *Spirit*. Potomac, Md.: Abbott.

Owen, H. 1990. *Leadership is*. Potomac, Md.: Abbott.

Owen, H. 1991. *Riding the tiger*. Potomac, Md: Abbott.

Pandit, S. 1988. Management excellence—An assessment of effective skills and practices in leading Indian businesses. Ph.D. diss., Sri Sathya Sai Institute of Higher Learning, Prasanthi Nilayam, India.

Pascale, R., and A. Athos. 1981. *The art of Japanese management*. New York: Warner.

Peck, M. S. 1982. *The road less traveled*. New York: Simon & Schuster.

Peck, M. S. 1987. *The different drum: Community making and peace*. New York: Simon & Schuster

Peters, T. 1987. *Thriving on chaos: Handbook for a management revolution*. New York: Knopf.

Peters, T., and R. Waterman. 1982. *In search of excellence*. New York: Harper & Row.

Pirsig, R. 1984. *Zen & the art of motorcycle maintenance: An inquiry into values*. New York: Bantam Books.

Pirsig, R. 1992. *Lila*. New York: Bantam Books.

Ramakrishna Ashram, ed. 1985. *Dharma for all*. Madras, India: Ramakrishnamath.

Renesch, J., ed. 1991. *New traditions in business: Spirit and leadership in the 21st century*. San Francisco: Berrett-Koehler.

Ritscher, J. 1992. *Achieving excellence: Creationg high-performance, spirited organizations.* Brookline, Mass.: Peak Dynamics.

Roerich, N. 1947. *Himalayas: Abode of light.* Bombay: Nalanda Publications.

Roof, J. 1991. *Pathways to God.* Faber, Va.: Leela.

Rose, A., and A. Auw. 1974. *Growing up human.* New York: Harper & Row.

Rowan, Roy. 1987. *The intuitive manager.* New York: Berkley Books.

Rukmini Studies. 1989. *The Vedantic approach to internal man management.* Madras, India: Srinagar Colony.

Sandweiss, S. 1975. *Sai Baba: The holy man and the psychiarist.* San Diego: Birth Day.

Sandweiss, S. 1985. *Spirit and the mind.* San Diego: Birth Day.

Sathya Sai Baba. n.d. *Indian culture and spirituality.* Prasanthi Nilayam, India: Sri Sathya Sai Books.

Senge, P. 1990. *The fifth discipline.* New York: Doubleday.

Shepard, H., and J. Hawley. 1974. *Life planning: Personal and organizational.* Washington, D.C.: National Training and Development Service Press.

Sivananda. 1986. *Concentration and meditation.* Shivanandanagar, India: Divine Life Society.

Spencer, S., and J. Adams. 1990. *Life changes: Growing through personal transitions.* San Luis Obispo, Calif.: Impact.

Sperry, R. 1991. Search of beliefs to live by consistent with science. *Zygon: Journal of Religion and Science* 26: 237–58.

Srivastava, A. K. 1980. *Bhagavad Gita: Economic development and management.* New Delhi: Abhinav Publications.

Srivastva, S., and Associates. 1988. *Executive integrity: The search or high human values in organizational life.* San Francisco: Jossey-Bass.

Stebbins, M., J. Hawley, and A. Rose. 1982. "Long-term action research." In *Organizational development in health care organizations,* edited by N. Margulies and J. Adams. Reading, Mass.: Addison-Wesley.

Subramaniam, K. 1989. *Mahabharata.* Bombay: Bharatiya Vidya Bhavan.

Talbot, M. 1991. *The holographic universe.* New York: HarperCollins.

Terhorst, P. 1988. *Cashing in on the American dream: How to retire at 35.* New York: Bantam Books.

Thomas, J. 1989. *Life is a game: Play it.* Cherry Valley, Calif.: Ontic Books.

Thomas, J. 1991. *Life is a challenge: Meet it.* Cherry Valley, Calif.: Ontic Books.

Trevelyan, G. 1986. *Summons to a high crusade.* Forres, Scotland: Findhorn Press.

Vaill, P. 1989. *Managing as a performing art.* San Francisco: Jossey-Bass.

Warner, J., ed. 1990. *Transformation of the heart.* York Beach, Maine: Samuel Weiser.

Watts, A. 1972. *The book: On the taboo against knowing who you are.* New York: Vintage.

Wheatley, M. 1992. *Leadership and the new science.* San Francisco: Berrett-Koehler.

Williams, A. 1989. *Developing corporate character.* San Francisco: Jossey-Bass.

Wolf, F. 1991. *The eagle's quest.* New York: Summit.

Yogananda, P. 1974. *Autobiography of a yogi.* Los Angeles: Self-Realization Fellowship.

Zaleznik, A. 1989. *The managerial mystique: Restoring leadership in business.* New York: Harper & Row.

INDEX